HAYWARDS ~~HEATH~~

Yesterday Remembered

by

LILIAN ROGERS

Dedicated to my parents

AMELIA AND GEORGE LANGRIDGE

"--------*Deposited upon the silent shore of memory images and precious thoughts that shall not die and cannot be destroyed.*" Wordsworth.

Printed and bound by RPM Reprographics Ltd. Chichester

Published March 1999 by Lilian Rogers

ISBN 0-95350-13-02

© Lilian Rogers, 1999

£6.50

Cover photograph by Edward Jacomb-Hood

PREFACE

Age sees the future 'through a glass darkly', yet might not that obscurity come from the shield that's raised — the shield of non-acceptance? So, turning the other way, the past is viewed with everything standing in clear focus. Let not the younger criticize, for Age hovers over all, and will, one day, descend.

CONTENTS

		Page
	Preface	iii
	Introduction	vii
	Start of letter	ix
1	The beginning	1 - 7
2	School days	8 - 19
3	Street traders	20 - 24
4	Treats and special days	25 - 30
5	A walk-about	31 - 42
6	Wide-eyed with wonder	43 - 47
7	Churches	48 - 51
8	Squeaky clean	52 - 55
9	Another walk	56 - 62
10	Shops	63 - 81
11	Changes	82 - 90
12	The way we were	91 - 96
13	War years	97 - 102
14	The Town grows	103 - 108
	Finish of letter	109

INTRODUCTION

This little booklet is <u>not</u> a history of the town, and any research has been from memories, postcards, photographs and newspaper cuttings, and there may well be disappointment for those who have different memories. My hope is that others of my generation may, for a while, relive some of their childhood, and younger readers be given a little idea of what life in Haywards Heath was like many years ago.

Acknowledgements. Patricia Avery M.A.
Donald Cashfield
Nora Green
Edward Jacomb-Hood B.Sc.,A.K.C., F.I.C.E.
Beryl Kent
Norman Langridge
David Vaughan F.S.V.A.

Ashlyn
56 Gower Road
Haywards Heath
West Sussex
RH16 4PN

Dear Haywards Heath,

Tonight I'm sitting down to start writing a letter to you. No, you don't know me, but I know you very well. You were my birthplace, you gave me my education, you gave me most of my living, and you have been my home for 80 years. You have altered of course, altered to suit the needs of your people, and you've grown too, my word you have grown! You have made mistakes over the years, of course you have, what town hasn't? But I love you warts and all. So many memories linger and now the time has come to put some of those memories on to paper lest they be lost for ever, and when I have done that, I will finish your letter - - - - -

CHAPTER 1

IN THE BEGINNING

"Begin at the beginning----" Lewis Carroll

Immediately the pushchair was turned at the top corner of Boltro Road, I knew we were heading for the station — the railway station which served this small quiet market town of Haywards Heath into which I had been born one month before the Great War drew to its close. Not that the station was to be our destination, the interest for me was in Market Place, that area between the bottom end of Boltro Road and the railway-arch over which the steam-trains thundered, for it was here, next to the station steps, and opposite, too, where the advertising hoardings were, and these were my delight. Here it was I became acquainted with the bowler-hatted dandy with his monocle and cane, advertising Sharp's toffee. There was the cheerful-looking shipwreck victim, too, sitting upon a floating crate of Bovril, with the caption, which had to be read to me, "Bovril prevents that sinking feeling". There were others of course, and periodically they would be changed.

Sometimes these pushchair outings were further afield, where there were other interests — Cuckfield, with Bedlam pond en route; Lindfield, with a larger pond, and its swans that glided toward us for the bread we offered. These outings were always determined by my mother, but when my school-teacher sister was home on holiday, she would offer a choice, and always the answer to her, "Where shall we go?", was the same, "To the rushing 'ridder'". To see this rushing river we would turn left under the Millgreen Road railway-arch, for a stream, now piped for development in that area. It was a modest stream, but apparently satisfied my obsession with water, an obsession which remains to this day. All walks were taken in the afternoon, mornings, for the housewife were for house-work and dinner preparation. Only once do I remember being out in the morning when under school age. Muster Green North, then being a through Road, meant five roads converged near The Sergison Arms, now the Dolphin, and in the centre was a curbed triangle of grass. Upon this was a gas lamp, surrounded by a slatted wooden seat, and it was here, with my mother, that I recall sitting, that morning we were out.

At four years old I was to experience my first car ride, when a great-uncle brought my mother and I home from the infirmary attached to the Cuckfield Union, the workhouse from which Cuckfield Hospital evolved. It was there where my paternal grandfather was dying. The journey over had been made by bus, Southdown in its early days, the bus being boarded from the Muster Green facing the top of Boltro Road. But first the pushchair was deposited with Mrs Catt, living in Cleveland Cottages, one of two at the rear of the Star, and backing on to Coleman's riding stables. The house, Clevelands, was opposite where Muster Court now stands, the grounds of the house extending to where the Westminster Bank was built.

Wet days meant days spent indoors, for the pushchairs had no hoods. Then I would hear nursery rhymes, poems, and listen to the adventures of Brer Rabbit and Bunkum Brown, bandit. My long-suffering mother would weary of reading, long before I became tired of listening.

But there is life before memory and, for me, that started one Tuesday afternoon in October 1918. Thinking his mother unwell seven year old Leslie was reluctant to return to school in the afternoon, but to school he had to go. Being acquainted, upon his home coming, with a baby sister, the observation to sister Edith was made that he thought it real mean of Nurse Biddle to bring that baby to his mum when she wasn't well. Charles at 20, was working away from home, Edith, two years younger, was soon to leave, so it is quite probable that our 44 year old father and 42 year old mother were not particularly overjoyed with this addition to the family, but unlike Leslie, attached no blame upon the midwife.

The house in which I was born was a semi-detached, three-bedroomed property very similar to others in the road, except that this pair had indoor lavatories. At this point, it might be of interest to compare property prices of way back with those of today. Mr Alfred Gower, from whom the Haywards Heath road was named, sold to a well known local architect and surveyor, Mr Arthur Pannett, a plot of freehold land, where Gower Road now is, then in the parish of Cuckfield. It had a frontage of 50ft. and a depth of 170ft. — enough for a pair of houses. The year was 1878, and the price £65. Twenty eight years later, in 1906, Mr Pannett was selling the same plot for £135, and on it, in the same year, was built a pair of houses by a local builder, Mr Thomas White. The pair, each with a tenant, was purchased by my father for £2,100 in 1923. One of the pair is today mine, bought with vacant possession in 1963 at £2,100. Altered and modernised, its valuation figure today is a six figure sum. Comparison between past and present property prices should be looked at alongside the then and now wages. I have no idea what my father was earning in 1923, the time of his house buying, but six years earlier in 1917, working for the Gower Road builders' firm of E. and J. Muzzell as foreman carpenter and joiner, he was earning 7d. an hour, a little over today's 2½p. and it was probably the same in 1923. So even with a mortgage, house buying was no small undertaking.

Back to the house in which I grew up. All windows were of the sash type and single-glazed, the lighting was by gas, electricity for the town was in the future, coming to our home in 1933. The gas was paid for by a shilling in the slot-meter, although for some folk it was a penny in the slot. A brass oil lamp or a candle saw us to bed.

There was no bathroom, so the bedrooms were equipped with marble-topped wash-stands, each with its china jug, basin, soap dish and tooth-brush holder. Towels hung upon a towel-horse, now once again fashionable. Water, heated downstairs, was carried up, and after use, taken down again in a white enamel slop-pail, and the pail came into use again for the emptying of the china chamber-pots. The bedsteads were iron, once again fashionable, and the front bedroom double mattress was a feather one, very comfortable, not good for the spine, and diabolical to shake up. A white honeycombed, cotton, bedspread covered each bed, and sheets were cotton, needing to be ironed with a heavy flat-iron heated on the kitchener. During winter our beds were warmed with either stone or rubber hot-water bottles. The aluminium bottle was to come later. All three bedrooms had open fireplaces, all unused.

Downstairs the bay-windowed sitting-room, known as the front room, was little used except at Christmas, little used that is, until my piano practice started, but it was home to the aspidistra, a hardy plant to be seen in the window of a good many houses at that time. The dining-room was known as the kitchen, and today's kitchen, the scullery, and in there was a shallow sink, a black iron gas-stove and a meat-safe. Also hanging there was a leather strop, upon which my father's 'cut-throat' razor was sharpened, and when he was shaving , none of us, not even my mother, would go to the scullery. Floor coverings were linoleum, obtainable again today.

There was no aesthetic planning for the rear garden. It was our little plot of land, worked in order to feed us, and grew our vegetables and fruit, was home to a few chicken and stored our supply of coal. Vegetables brought in were cleaned, cooked and eaten straight away, fruit not for immediate use was bottled or made into jam or jelly, and surplus eggs preserved in an earthenware crock of water-glass, an operation known as 'putting eggs down'. My memory of the interior of the chicken-house is very clear, for Leslie locked me in, intending immediate release. Unfortunately his attention was directed elsewhere and I was forgotten until tea time. A superb reason for a psychiatrist today, to attribute any claustrophobic tendencies I might have — but I have none.

Quite intentionally the kitchen has been left to the end, not because it was of no importance, far from it, for it was the very hub of the house, the place where, when not in bed, all of our indoor hours were spent, our living-room, as a family. Here was the dining-table, the sideboard, the dresser, the little corner cupboard, all hand-made by my father at the start of his married life. Here too, was the kitchener, a 'Lambert', a black iron coal-fired range, with a small boiler at the side, which needed to be filled by hand, and never to be allowed to get empty when the fire was alight. Over the range was a sturdy iron rack, where clothes were aired, a brass-topped nursery-guard stood before the hearth, and in front of that, on the floor a rag rug of my mother's making, by hooking small strips of material through hessian. At one time Americans were paying a high price for this type of rug. Cooking was done in here, and here was kept and used my mother's sewing machine. Here she would sit on winter evenings, her knitting needles clicking, while any wool needed for re-use was wound around a piece of wood, and would be placed over a steaming, lidless kettle, to remove its crinkle. My father would sit, book in hand, reading, but his many commitments often took him from home in the evenings. One obituary notice spoke of him as a prominent Haywards Heath resident. I have been told he was an excellent after-dinner speaker. When he died, I missed him very, very much. Board games were played here, and while Leslie worked at his fretwork, I would knit, do raffia work, or a jigsaw puzzle, made with wooden pieces, not cardboard as today. Winter mornings were cold for breakfasts, for there was no heat till the ashes were removed and the kitchener fire laid and lit. What bliss there was when a 'Valor' oil stove came into the home, but that was later on.

The town had smaller houses, larger ones too, though many of the latter we never saw, for they were concealed behind high fences and hedges, ensuring complete privacy for their occupants. Tradesmen had their own entrance leading to the back door. Many of these houses have now been demolished and it would be impracticable to include them all, but to name a few, will give an understanding of the change as the population grew and the need for more living accommodation increased. Haute Terre at the top end of Franklyn Road went for a housing estate; Clevelands on the Muster Green went for flats, Muster Court. The houses Winnals, Jireh, and Ormerod demolished, the names being retained for the flats erected upon their respective sites. Petlands, at the top end of Oathall Road, with grounds reaching to Heyworth School in New England Road, came down in 1955 making way for the flats, Hazelgrove Gardens. Oakwood Road, at one time private, was opened up for development, and both Oakwood and Great Haywards went, but Great Haywards farmhouse remains. Beech Hurst, bequeathed to the town by the late Mr W Yapp, was pulled down, the name living on in the beautiful recreational centre formed from its grounds; Brent Eleigh lost its grounds in South Road for commercial development in the 30's, the house remaining until the precinct project. Elfinsward on the corner of Bolnore Road pulled down and our police headquarters occupy the site; Trubweeke in Heath Road demolished for our Health Centre, regrettably losing its name, for as Trubwick it is shown as early as 1638 on the manorial map.

Some still remain, Oaklands, much enlarged, as our Council offices; Birch House as the Birch Hotel; Beechmont — one time Franklyns — in the Princess Royal Hospital complex; and Bolnore and Butler's Green House both suitably adapted as flats.

Clevelands, Muster Green, demolished 1959 for Muster Court flats

Oakwood, Oakwood Road, off Muster Green

CHAPTER 2

SCHOOL DAYS

"When all the world is young, lads" Charles Kingsley

The town was well served for fee-paying schools. To name but a few, there was Farlington in Oathall Road and Trevelyan in Church Road both for girls, while boys were at Brunswick in Oathall Road, and Parkfield on the corner of Isaac's Lane — now Downlands Park nursing home — , Sharrow in Church Road, and Hillcrest in Heath Road and Mount St Joseph's for girls and small boys, in Hazelgrove Road.

Three schools within a distance of a ¼ mile stood in South Road. On the corner of Church Road was the elementary, Church of England school of St Wilfrid. Further along, opposite the entrance to Haywards Road, stood a County School for Girls, and cheek by jowl with that, an elementary Council school. The first and third were co-educational, for children from the age of 5 to the school-leaving age of 14.

In September 1923 I was off to the Council School. There was no gradual introduction to school life, one day we were at home, the next at school from 9 in the morning until 4 o'clock, with a dinner break of 1¾ hours. A week or so before, I had been taken there, met the headmaster Mr Owen Freestone, and been accepted as a pupil for the lower infants class. On that first day my mother accompanied me in the morning, and upon her insistence, again in the afternoon, and from then on I was on my own. The South Road of today bears no resemblance to that of 1923, with its leisurely horse-drawn traffic and the occasional car, quite unable to attain the speed of today's traffic.

It was a brick built, one storeyed school, well lit, well ventilated, well heated. Built in 1907 with class-rooms leading off a central corridor, it had been enlarged prior to my going, and was to be again, after I had left. It stood concealed from the road, by a low wall, and high railings, backed by tall evergreens. Both the entrances and playgrounds were separate for boys and girls, but the class-rooms were shared. When the bell summoned us for lessons, straight lines were formed under the teacher's direction, and with no talking, we were marshalled into school, where we sat, arms folded, at double desks each with inkwell. Caning was an accepted custom for any misdemeanour, but for boys only. Though the drawing lessons had no relation to art, nor the singing to music, and learning was by rote, the basic subjects were taught well. All were fine teachers there — all, that is, except one, who was unable to maintain discipline or teach, without ruling by fear, and when that needs to be done, the teacher is in the wrong profession. That woman <u>certainly</u> was.

Even though there may have been schools where their homes were, pupils were coming to the Haywards Heath one from Wivelsfield Green, Ditchling, Burgess Hill, Cuckfield, Handcross and Dane Hill. Provision was made for their bicycles, and the sandwiches brought with them were eaten in the corridor, for there were no school dinners. That same corridor became the class-room for the boys' carpentry lessons. The girls' cookery class was shared with girls from St Wilfrid's School, the latter having no cookery-room.

A doctor and dentist paid visits periodically. The dentist, a dour man, held surgery in the Co-op hall, over the shop in Sussex Road, his dental chair being placed in the bay window. Measles, Mumps, German measles, whooping cough, chicken-pox, and scarlet fever all spread rapidly, and with each child absent for some six weeks, the school attendance figure was low, sometimes necessitating the closure of the school.

In South Rd: opposite Haywards, hidden behind wall, railings and trees, stood the Council School, its site now covered with shops.

Next to it, and also well hidden, the County School for Girls

Our two school managers were Mr Harry Plummer and Mr George Hilton, the latter always sharing with us his windfall apples.

In addition to no dinners, there were no uniforms, no morning assembly, no house scheme, no prefects, no projects, no home-work, no parent-teacher associations and no overseas holidays. There was, however, school milk which was introduced 1928/29, for which we paid ½d. for ⅓ pint.

From the Council School came my introduction to both Dickens and Shakespeare, and it was there I met Norman — Norman Harmer, who surreptitiously passed me coded notes, in class. The present he gave me, I have still. I hope life has been good to him.

I left to go to the County School, and I did so with no regrets.

One September morning in 1932 I walked past the Council School and through the open double gates of the school next to it, the Haywards Heath County School for Girls, opposite the Haywards Road entrance. It stood behind iron railings, screened from the road by evergreen shrubs and trees. Built for a private residence, it had later become a private school for boys, "Heathmere", until, in 1905, it was purchased by the East Sussex Local Education Authority, with the adjacent plot of land. Upon this site was to be built, and opened in 1907, a Council School, the very one I had just left. The "Heathmere" building was used for a Girls' Pupil Teacher Centre, sharing it for two years with the children who were to be admitted to the Council School from an overcrowded St Wilfrid's School. By the time I was going there it had ceased to be a school solely for pupil teachers, admission being by County scholarship or by a fee of £14 yearly, payable each term at £4. 13s. 4d.

Here we wore a uniform, a navy-blue gym-slip, white blouse, black stockings, indoor and outdoor shoes both black leather, a school tie. There was a uniform hat, felt in winter, Panama in summer, with a hat-band of the school colours, navy-blue coat or blazer. There were also gloves to be worn, not only in winter, but with our uniform summer dresses, and woebetide anybody seen without their gloves. A white dress had to be worn for our yearly speech day, held in the public hall. There were three 'houses', Stuart, Tudor and Windsor, and a school motto, "Noblesse Oblige" — privilege entails responsibility and this rule of conduct I have endeavoured to live by ever since, and if it has been impossible to shoulder the responsibility, then the accompanying privilege has been surrendered.

The Education Authority had purchased some land at Oathall Park, where now stands Oathall Community College, and here were our playing fields to where we walked in a crocodile once a week. Discipline was strict at this school — no talking on the stairs, and always a prefect on cloakroom duty to maintain good behaviour. At the start of a lesson, one girl would open the door for the entry of a mistress and close it behind her, while the whole class would stand until told to sit. A small misdemeanour would bring an order-mark to the whole form, while a larger one would earn for the individual a black conduct-mark. Reports on our work for the term were given in sealed envelopes addressed to our parents, for us to take home unopened. There came the day when mine was found to be opened, and I was nearly expelled. Not only had I disobeyed, but I had opened a missive, addressed to somebody else, and to say I was reprimanded by the headmistress, would be an understatement. My awful deed was declared by her at assembly the next morning, and the school was told of my black mark. That report, and the one for the following term, reached my parents through the post, after which, apparently, I could be trusted.

After a stay of two years at that school, it closed, with the opening of the Hove County School for Girls. For all its strict discipline, it was at the Haywards Heath County School where I was happiest and where I learnt so much, and I have a lot for which to thank the headmistress, Miss A. Louise Stevens, and her staff. On leaving, Miss

Stevens opened a fee-paying school at St Clair, a private residence at the northern end of Perrymount Road, now demolished. It was here some of the South Road pupils went, for others it meant the termination of their schooling, and forty six, both scholarship and fee-paying pupils, were transferred to the new school at Hove. Unfortunately I was included in that number.

As five-year olds there were games played in the school playground under the supervision of a teacher, which were part of the curriculum and quite separate from games at playtime. "What's the time, Mr Wolf?", "The farmer's in his den", and "Crusts and crumbs", were a few of them. When older, the boys played football and cricket, with home matches played in Victoria Park and away matches at other venues. For the girls it was stoolball and netball.

Games played at school playtime were of our own choosing, although there were always in both playgrounds, two teachers on duty. There were ball games, for which the girls' sloping play area was not too suitable. Of chasing games there was a variety, from the simple one of 'Tag' to 'Chain-tag', or as we called it, 'Ram-ram'. First of all, the one to chase, termed 'He', had to be chosen, so a circle would be formed each girl holding out both hands palms upward. One would stand in the centre, touching in turn each of the outstretched hands to the rhythm of a rhyme such as:-

"My father made a horse's shoe,
How many nails did he put through?"
"Five (or whatever number was chosen)
The number chosen was then counted out on the
outstretched hands.

However, if the girl in the centre wasn't happy with the end result, she would extend her counting with the words:-

"And that very one that I touch last must surelye be 'Old Man'".

Then if she still wasn't satisfied she would add the words, "O.U.T. spells out", and at last the chasing game would commence. 'Old Man' was another term for 'He'— the chaser; and that word 'surelye' is a Sussex one meaning surely, but with a greater emphasis. There were several of these rhymes for 'counting out', as we called it.

In the game of Ram-ram, when the chaser touched, — or 'caught' we called it, — one of the runners-away, they both would join hands, and continue the chase, and with enough girls playing, the chain could be a long one. The girls' playground was shared with the five-year old girls and boys, and a herd of fourteen-year olds swooping down upon them and knocking them over, as their last victim was chased, must have terrified the little mites. Probably there were tears at home, bringing complaints from their parents, causing the headmaster, Mr Freestone, to bar the playing of the game of Ram-ram. So we settled for Tag, and in this game if one being chased needed a respite, the first and second fingers would be crossed as she shouted, "Feinites". I cannot vouch for the spelling of that word, any more than I can in a game we played , when we sang, "The big ship sailed o'er the Ally ally-o." It was the game itself that was important, and the games were passed down from older sisters and never seen written.

We skipped, either individually, or with a longer rope needing to be held by a girl each end and several could skip together. Sometimes two long ropes would be used, one being turned in a clockwise direction, the other in an anti-clockwise. It was known as French skipping, and the knack of being able to do it was to adopt a very slight hip movement from side to side.

With a leather-boot lace securely fastened to a stick, we whipped our wooden tops into action, with varieties which included mushroom and carrot. There were games played with marbles, either with a board or without, and these were enjoyed, too, by the boys in their playground, as were games with conkers.

Probably our proximity to the park meant there was little playing in the road. Very occasionally if it wasn't quite bedtime, we would use the road for a game of Statues, Cups and Saucers or Hopscotch. The latter needed a chalk tracing on the road surface, and if this is what we had done, then equipped with a stiff broom and a bucket of water, I had to efface it before going in. We girls bowled our wooden hoops along the pavements, the boys having iron ones, and while the girls had a wooden stick, the boys had an iron skid to control it, and those skids cost a halfpenny.

I learnt in the home why the local park was named Victoria Park. Bought, as a field, from Mr Arthur Pannett, by public subscription, it was the town's memorial to the Queen's Diamond Jubilee. But to we children it was simply the park, and never did we go along to it, or down to it, or simply to it, always *up* to it. "Let's go *up* the park", we would say, and on the four week school holiday in the summer, that's where we were practically all day, keeping an eye on St Wilfrid's church clock, to get home in time for dinner, tea and again at bed-time. There were then gates at both South Road and Park Road entrances, the former opening on to the wide path we called the promenade.

On the south side of the park's frontage stood the fire station, its date of origin plain to see on the front brick-work — 1903. Here were also the council offices prior to their move to Oaklands, and public toilets before their re-siting in the 1950's, on to the promenade. This was done at the suggestion of Mr Cyril Snell, the council's chairman, causing the toilets to be dubbed Snell's Folly.

The park was much less attractive than it is today, being not much more than grass and oak trees. There was one more tennis court, and a smaller level, where we watched the Asters in their pink dresses and the Bluebells wearing blue, play stool-ball. Surrounded by low shrubs and iron railings was the larchwood bandstand, and even as children we had pride in our Haywards Heath Town Prize Band playing under the baton of Mr W.Bosley.

We had no paddling-pool, or play equipment, though for a time, there was a sand-pit, but due to fouling by dog or child, its life was short. There was a refreshment kiosk run by Mrs Stubbs, wife of the park-keeper: and, of course, there was the plantation, known to us as the 'planny'. It was not then landscaped, but was a rough grassy surface, where blackberry bushes abounded and over a hundred larch trees grew, but many of the latter, suffering from heart-rot, had to be felled. There was a hollow we thought deep, seen today we would probably show surprise at its lack of depth, but going there one day, we found a larch tree straddling it and its elasticity gave a slight trampoline effect as we sat astride. What fun we had with it, but alas it was to be there only one summer. When tired of our play we would quite often shun the seats in favour of sitting upon a fence from where we could wave to the occupants of the passing steam trains. The plantation was formed by earth excavated in 1841 with the construction of the railway line, and trees planted to hold the earth in place.

With the coming of the football season, the park gates would be closed on Saturdays, opened only for payment. We girls were disconsolate. "Why do they do this to us? It's our park. It's not fair", we complained bitterly. Tarpaulin was erected above the South Road hedge to prevent any endeavouring to watch the game without paying, but to some this presented no problem. The mental hospital patients who were well enough to be allowed to come into the town on Saturday afternoons and wished to watch the game, quite simply leaned on the top of the tarpaulin to get it down to below eye-level.

One Saturday morning I heard good news from a girl living near me, Dorothy Satchwell, blonde, and on the day in question, wearing a

Showing both the larchwood band-stand erected by voluntary labour in 1920, and the promenade minus public toilets.

The "planny" of larch trees, planted on earth excavated from the nearby railway tunnel

pretty primrose yellow dress, gathered at the waist and full skirted. "Meet me at the Park Road entrance at 3 o'clock and I'll show you how to get into the park when it's locked", she said. I was there before her and viewed those locked double gates, iron and sturdy and painted a mat, dark red. Some seven inches from the top, a rail went across the width of each gate, and above the rail, spikes. Dorothy arrived. "Watch me", she said, in a business-like manner. I watched. One plimsolled foot was placed on the rail, and I can remember, even now, noticing the very fine, fair hairs upon her shapely, outstretched leg. Then, quick as lightning, she hurled herself up and over, her full skirt billowing out in the air. It was a sickening noise as the spike ripped her skirt from waist to hem. I can't recall her getting back to my side of the gate, but she must have done, for together we walked to our respective homes, not a word being spoken between us, neither did we ever mention it afterwards. I suppose there are some events which demand silence, but I have wished many times since that I had accompanied her home. Would it have softened the blow? Perhaps not. We were to find another way of getting in to the park, less risky.

Muster Green was without its war memorial until 1924, when it was unveiled by Lord Leconfield on November 30th its seven-and-a-half tons of granite being brought from Penryn in Cornwall. It was also minus the lovely flower-beds we enjoy today. Being enclosed it was not a play area for us, but occasionally, passing by in the Spring, we would pause a while to make a daisy-chain, or pick a buttercup for, "He loves me; he loves me not". In 1979 it was designated a conservation area.

Today we may read of a property on the market as, "Overlooking Clair Park", and I am left to wonder whether a prospective buyer really finds that more attractive than the same house "Commanding a view of the Recreation Ground". Police reports have been known to read of incidents having occurred in Clair Park, so maybe there has been a name change from its original Heath Recreation Ground, but I think not. Affectionately it was curtailed to the rec', and to those who spent their childhood in the town, that is how it is still known.

On many a Saturday afternoon in the cricket season, it was to the 'rec' I went with my parents, for having been a cricketer, my father loved to watch a game. For me the appeal was the smell from any pipe-smoking spectators, and so evocative is smell, that only to be near a pipe-smoker today, takes me back to the 'rec' on a sunny afternoon, with a game of cricket in progress.

Cricket Week in the Recreation Ground

CHAPTER 3

STREET TRADERS

"He's the Man Who Delivers the Goods"   Walt Mason

There were daily deliveries to the road, from the postman, the milkman and the baker's roundsman. There were three postal deliveries, two in the morning, one in the afternoon, brought by the postman, his uniform hat peaked both front and back. Letters cost 1½d. to send, postcards 1d. and at Christmas time, if our cards were in an unsealed envelope and bore no more than five words of greeting, they went for a ½d. Parcels were delivered from a large, red, wicker basket on wheels, hand-pushed.

The two milkmen remembered are Mr Charlie Holden and Mr Gus Butler. Mr Holden, bringing milk from Harlands Farm, stood behind the churn in a two-wheeled milk-cart, looking like a charioteer, as he drove the little well-groomed horse. Mr Butler, who supplied our family with milk, had a double-fronted shop with a dairy at the rear in South Road, next but one, on the lower side of the Congregational Church, now United Reformed. In one window stood a large milk-bowl, in the other, a golden cow. His milk churn was pushed in a milk pram, two large wheels at the rear, a smaller one in the front. His arrival at the back door with a large milk-can was always announced by a yodel, and the milk was ladled into our china jug by long-armed measuring ladles, suspended from the can by their ends being hooked over the rim. Until the 1920's milk was neither pasteurised nor bottled, and when the Co-operative Stores carried out a door-to-door canvass of its members promoting this, my mother was won over. The metal milk-top came later, at first a cardboard circle fitted into the bottle top, having in its centre a small circle, just big enough to be pushed in by a finger-tip, so that milk could be poured.

Mr Charlie Holden in Harlands Farm milk-cart

Co-op delivery van.

There was probably a name in the bakery trade for the large, lidded box on wheels that was pushed by both Mr Percy Woodland and Mr Jack Jury at different times to bring our Co-op bread. Before coming to the door, he would fill a stout basket with a selection of bread and cakes, and had a good idea of the needs of each customer.

Our house refuse was collected weekly by two men in a horse-drawn cart. As it was an open cart, it was smelly, and from my mother I received strict instructions about going by it. Approaching, a deep breath was to be taken, then holding it, I was to rush by the cart at speed, only then could I exhale and breath normally again.

With no central heating, coal-carts were more conspicuous, horse-drawn of course, as was the cart of the rag-and-bone man. Occasionally a rabbit skin collector would call, giving a penny or two for each skin, and when the price rose to threepence, I remember the excited joy of one house-wife, as she said to my mother, "Fancy, threepence for a rabbit-skin!" There were men who came to the door with very heavy suitcases of haberdashery, seeming so pleased if an item or two were purchased. Sometimes there would be a band, playing as it walked the streets, collecting money and children, and, following the first world war, it was quite usual to see disabled ex-service men busking, in an endeavour to augment a small pension, and a penny would be gratefully accepted.

There were two yearly visitors to the road, one in the spring, the other in the winter. Spring would bring the Dutch onion man, always wearing a navy blue beret, strings of onions hanging from the handlebars of his bicycle and every winter came the muffin-man, his appearance being heralded by the ringing of a hand-bell. He would walk slowly along the pavement, always wearing a green baize apron, a tray of muffins on his head, and if my mother bought some, then out would come the long-handled wire toasting-fork and they would be toasted before the open fire, buttered, and eaten for tea.

Every Saturday brought Mr Jerry Slater from Brighton, to sell fruit, and if he found, by the time he reached Haywards Road, he was a little late, he would turn in the direction of Gower Road and give a mighty shout, to tell us he was on his way. Quite often he would ask my mother if she would take a couple of orange-boxes out of his way, and he would put in any specked oranges which he would never offer for sale. The wood of the boxes fed the copper on washing-day, and the specked oranges were eatable. Oranges were wrapped in white tissue paper, printed in colour with the source of their origin, and I collected these, mounting them in a scrap book. Even before adolescence they had gone as rubbish, along with the cigarette-card albums and other collectables of that time, which have now become collectable again, and expensive. If only we had known! A knife and scissor grinder also visited at regular intervals.

A glut of plums would bring a Brighton dealer to the town in his motorised transport, and reaching the top of the road, he would cup both hands around his mouth to announce his presence. A glut meant a drop in price for grower, merchant and customer, and at the price they were, no paper bags were going to be supplied, so the shout brought housewives out into the road with bowls and basins. The plums would then be bottled or made into jam, but first a few put aside for a plum pie.

It was the same procedure for a glut of herrings, dishes and plates taking the place of the bowls and basins. Then coming in from afternoon school, I would be met with that lovely smell of herrings being soused in the oven, and I knew just what I would hear from my mother, "Don't take off your coat; go and get a bay-leaf." This little operation necessitated my going to Hazelgrove Road, and in the front garden, just behind the hedge of Mr Plummer's house, "Lyntonville", — one of the houses demolished for the precinct project — stood a bay tree, its leaves high up, but overhanging the pavement. I needed to walk further up the hill, then turn and rush down and with a mighty leap to the boughs to grab and obtain one leaf. It was to me very confusing, for we had all been brought up to know right from wrong, and stealing was definitely a wrong. Indeed, hadn't my mother so often quoted her school-teacher, "To steal a pin is as big a sin as if it were a larger thing". Yet I was sent to steal a bay-leaf. I came to the conclusion that while the theft of pins fell into a sin category, bay-leaves didn't.

From so much horse-drawn transport there was, quite often a by-product, and then could be seen dextrous action with shovel and bucket. At home we were well supplied, as Leslie, for a time, equipped with barrow and shovel, did a Saturday morning tour, once allowing me to accompany him, which I felt was a great honour. Everybody's rhubarb thrived.

A rural view of Hazelgrove Road

CHAPTER 4

TREATS AND SPECIAL DAYS

"----those heavenly days that cannot die"   William Wordsworth

The approach to Christmas was shorter than it is today, and the pressure to buy, much less, with no television commercials and fewer local shops. Why cry, "Buy!, buy!" when there is little money with which to do so? We looked forward to the shop windows being decorated, and when they were, there was an air of excitement. One year Father Christmas found his way to Cobb's stores, and I remember the Co-operative hall being transformed into a veritable wonderland of toys. Strips of different coloured paper were bought, and from these, with a little flour-paste, paper chains were made to adorn the kitchen. Until each married, Charles and Edith would be home for Christmas, and their home-coming was eagerly anticipated.

The door of the front room was locked, my mother being guardian of the key, but Christmas morning, the content of the stocking unwrapped and breakfast over, the door was opened to reveal the room's glory. Paper decorations hung gaily, no home-made affair these, but purchased years before, and after every Christmas taken down with care, folded and boxed, to be brought out and used again the following year. There were apples, oranges, tangerines, figs, dates, dishes of mixed nuts and sweets, not forgetting the presents, and an open fire giving a warm welcome. For dinner there would be roast chicken, a dish much less on the menu than it is today, and Christmas pudding would follow, as would the iced and decorated cake at tea-time, both home-made by my mother while I was at school and kept a secret. Only once was there a Christmas tree.

Christmas over, there would be a party for me, and a little later a visit to a Brighton pantomime — none then being held locally. The year of the Christmas tree, no mention was made of the visit, and unable to curb my impatience any longer, asked when we might be going, to receive my mother's quick reply, "We're not, you had a Christmas tree." One small girl found out that you don't have the moon and the stars. The disappointment was hard to bear, for had the choice been mine, the pantomime would have won, and the frustration remained with me for a long time. It was years later while a patient in hospital, that I met a woman, whom as a girl, had come to that particular party, and there in the ward, she reminisced, telling me how much she had enjoyed it. She spoke of that Christmas tree, and the present from it — a bag of nuts: and as she told of it, she was savouring once again all the pleasure it had meant to her, and I thought of how I had loathed that tree for robbing me of the pantomime. Suddenly I felt very, very humble.

Birthdays were celebrated with a few friends to tea, a birthday cake, home-made, and presents.

Sunday schools were well attended, and yearly there were two treats, and they were known as treats, for indeed, this is what they were. In the Congregational Sunday School, the winter one took the form of a tea in the church hall, which was decorated, complete with a Christmas tree, and the tea was followed by a scholars' concert, the mums and dads forming the audience. For this we had rehearsed, and for one glorious hour felt we were celebrities. Concert over, home we went, each child with an orange.

The summer treat took us to the seaside, Bexhill, Worthing, Eastbourne or Brighton. We made the journey with the Sussex Road Primitive Methodists and the Perrymount Road Wesleyans, and there were enough of us to merit the closure of the Council School for the day, and to have a special train solely for us — a steam train of course. The more fortunate of us boarded the train equipped with a packet of cellophane wrapped multi-coloured streamers to hold from the carriage window when the train gained momentum. The less fortunate were soon to acquire some by making a grab as they streamed temptingly past their window from the adjacent one, and the shouts of glee from the delighted captors, mingled with the cries of dismay from the robbed, left holding a much shorter streamer.

Our sandwiches, taken with us, were eaten on the beach, and strict instructions were given re the time and venue for the tea. This was always held in a church hall, the ladies of that particular church being our hostesses. However, one memorable year, although held in a church hall, the food was from caterers, and we were duly impressed by the waiters who served us. At the conclusion of the tea, we were each served with a cream-meringue, which for a good many, if not all of us, was something never previously tasted. With hindsight those waiters cannot have been overjoyed at having to wait upon a hoard of excitable, noisy, hungry children. All good things come to an end, and after the tea, we made our way to the station, happy, tired and sunburnt, to relive it all again later at home, as an account of the day was given to those who hadn't been. Some may have been mislaid during the day, but none were ever lost.

While at the Council School there weren't many who would have spent a holiday away, for though Bank Holidays were introduced in 1871, it was not until 1938 that paid holidays became law. So for two successive years, when my mother and I enjoyed a holiday in a lovely little cottage on the Rendell estate in east Brighton, my father was unable to join us. However, he came at weekends, as did the rest of the family in turn. Whether one of those two years was a leap year, I know not, but with all the gravity of an eight or nine years old, tackling such a serious subject, I did ask the gardener, Mr Keene, if he would wait for me to grow up, as I wanted to marry him. They were lovely holidays, and I thought at the time, that if heaven was going to be like that, then I'd be happy to go.

Normally there would be a summer visit to the seaside for the day. Scanning the daily paper my mother would find the tide's movement at London Bridge, then by either adding or subtracting time, she would be able to define when it would be low or high at Brighton. Having arrived there by train, a tram would be boarded, and sitting upstairs, we would be taken to the Old Steine, but before arrival I would sit looking neither right nor left, but staring ahead, to catch that first glimpse of the water. Then caring nothing for the indulgent smiles of other passengers, or my mother's look of slight embarrassment, my high-pitched, excited voice would shriek, "Mum, I can see the sea".

Previously a town dweller, but a great lover of the country-side, my mother would look with yearning toward the distant South Downs, but how to get to them we didn't know, until somebody living in the road, went there. We were told a No. 23 Southdown bus would get us to Ditchling, but after that there was a long , long walk. The next Bank Holiday saw sandwiches and flasks of tea being packed, for we were going to head toward the Downs, and if we didn't reach them, well at least we would have been out in the fresh air. So we took the double-decker bus to Ditchling and all being good walkers were agreeably surprised to reach the foot of the hills, thinking nothing of the distance.

We climbed; no cars, no ice-cream van, and very few people; the silence was breath-taking, as was the view from the Beacon. How we wished we had done this earlier. We saw a lark rise from among the chalk-hill blue butterflies, we came across a dew pond, we met a shepherd, and we walked over to Clayton, making close acquaintance with Jack and Jill, the two windmills, before dropping down to the road to get a bus home. Young as I was, it was there on the Downs that a feeling of awe was sensed, and the sheer beauty of Sussex took hold of me, and has never let go. That visit was to be the first of many. To a certain extent these outings may be seen as a distancing from Haywards Heath, but their inclusion will serve to highlight the importance of the pleasure derived from the visits to the sea and the Downs, both so near home.

There were several annual events to be enjoyed, one of which was the Whit Monday Fête. Organised to aid the local hospital and others in Brighton, the fête was comprised of stalls, sideshows and a funfair, and took place in the park. An 1896 cutting of the July Flower Show, shows it as a one-day event, but in my youth it took place over two days, always a Wednesday and a Thursday, and apart from wonderful flower and plant displays, there was a gymkhana. Being held in the park, both St Wilfrid's School and the Council school were near enough to suffer from the noise of the show, especially from the funfair, and the Council school closed, losing two days from the summer holiday. I would think it probable that the other school did the same. The band played in the little larchwood bandstand, which had been built in 1920 from the trees in the plantation, and the whole show was important enough to receive coverage in the Daily Telegraph. One year I wasn't to go to the Flower Show for a reason long forgotten, but I went to the park gate, and there was a laddie who also hadn't the six pence for admission. "I know a way to get in", he said. Together we ran at speed down Mr Pratt's path at the side of his butcher's shop, and passing his stabled horse, we came out to the plantation and dropped down into the park, where we parted company. I never knew the identity of my knight in shining armour, but had he, after all, done so much for me? Where is the fun of the fair with no money to spend? Yet, ever after, there was a feeling of satisfaction in knowing that it was indeed possible to gain access to the park though the gates be locked. It was done only that once, for I knew should my parents happen to hear of that little escapade, there would be big trouble for me.

There was a much smaller event held annually for the children of Co-op members, and was simply races and a tea. The first time I went, about the age of four, it was held on land in Oathall Road, long since built upon, thereafter the event took place in the park. There was no charge, admission being by ticket available from the cash desk at the shop in Sussex Road, and my mother was always most adamant, that I obtained that ticket myself. Her "If you don't want to get that ticket, then you don't go", was really meant, and in later life I have had cause to be thankful that in so many ways I was made to be independent.

The words went around the Council School like wild-fire, "Beech Hurst is open". Once a year, Mr W. Yapp, the owner of the house, opened his grounds to the public, and it was an event we joyfully anticipated. Getting there in the evening, we behaved with decorum, in fact, tending to be somewhat overawed by these grounds so much larger than our back gardens. Only fairly recently have I learnt it was a fund-raising event for the Alexandra Rose Day Nurses Fund, and I believe all of we children were ignorant of this, and feel now that I would have had some small contribution to take, had my parents known.

The Country Market was an annual event, in aid of our local hospital. Before the death of Mr Yapp, it was held, with his permission, on land at Beech Hurst, his home. I must admit to never going as a child, and by the time I attended it was being held in the grounds of the hospital.

August brought the fair every year to Lindfield Common — the cheap-jacks, the sideshows, the fortune-tellers, the shooting-galleries, the confetti-seller, the stalls, the coconut shies, the fish and chip van, the swings, the roundabout. Above all of it, the lights, the noise of shouting, of music, of laughter, and the smell of trodden grass. My father excelled at the coconut shy, and some were given away, and some brought home, but it's not an easy task to carry home roly-poly coconuts, and in my mind's eye even now, I see my mother wriggling out of her waist-slip, while walking home, to pick it up and wrap it around those coconuts. One year I was no help with the carrying of them, for my arms were full with a double-jointed doll won by my mother. We walked each way to and from the fair, until Mr Jessett ran a charabanc service at sixpence each way, then sometimes we would have a ride home, but had he just moved off with a full load, we would walk. Once, walking home, we saw glow worms, and in my mind they are for ever linked with Lindfield Fair.

CHAPTER 5

A WALK-ABOUT

"What is this life if, full of care, we have no time to stand and stare?"
William H Davies

The road name plates of the town were enamelled on metal, the background a royal blue, the name itself in white, some may still be seen today. The Haywards Heath and District Gas Company supplied our gas, and it was the job of a lamplighter to light the gas-lamps at dusk, returning later at night to extinguish them. R.L.Stevenson's poem, "The Lamplighter", learnt at school, was well within our comprehension.

"For every night at tea-time and before you take your seat,
With lantern and with ladder, he comes posting up the street."

Not until the late 1930's did our local government authority become the Cuckfield Urban District Council, so the notice boards on the Muster Green, in the park and recreation ground, listing prohibitions in each of these areas, were headed Haywards Heath Urban District Council.

There were twittens in the town, paths connecting two roads. Like the word 'surelye' in a previous chapter, twitten is a Sussex word, and as natives of that county, we swallow the two central letter t's and make it a twi'en. St John's Road was Asylum Twitten, another linking South and Gower Roads is still being used, although slightly altered. At the South Road end stood our Public Hall, brick built, and erected in 1889, a terra-cotta eagle standing high on the roof. Post-war modernisation of the hall saw the eagle's removal, and a change of name to Sussex Hall.

Sussex Square, with the eagle high on the Public Hall. Note the wooden bicycle stand on the forecourt of Muzzell and Hilton's shop.

The new name for the Public Hall after post war modernisation, later its site covered by an extension to Sainsbury's.

St Wilfrid's Gymnasium Club.

Left to right. Back row. Rev'd F.Du Boulay. Mr H.Mynott. Miss N.Willson

Middle Row. J.Gasson. H.Mitchell. R.Howard. F.Cowdrey.

Front Row. G.Swaysland. G.Holmes. R.Cowdrey.

Under both names it served the community well as a venue for meetings and social occasions. Two postcards in my collection show it as a military hospital in the 1914-18 War, one showing the large red cross, the other, wounded and nurses on the forecourt. In 1920 those who had served in that war were welcomed home with a dinner served in the hall. The venue was the same for those returning from the 1939-45 war, when the welcome home was an evening meal followed by a show. The latter I attended, but not then having been bitten by the collecting bug, no invitation or menu was kept. In 1974 a new community centre, Clair Hall in Perrymount Road was opened, and the Sussex Hall was no more.

At the Gower Road end of the twitten stood the Church Lads Brigade Hall, shortened to C.L.B.hall, erected in 1898, a corrugated iron building, for the Haywards Heath Company of the brigade. In 1917 it was commandeered for a hospital, and the Company was disbanded for the duration, and it seems likely never to have continued after the war. Although, unlike the Public Hall, it had no stage, it was certainly very much used for a variety of purposes, one of which was St Wilfrid's Gymnastic Club. The Instructor was Mr H. Mynott, the president the Rev'd F. Du Boulay and the pianist Miss N. Willson. They were certainly well trained lads, for in 1933, they were winners of the Margesson Cup outright and many were the displays they gave at outdoor functions. The hall, demolished in 1965, made way for the Gower Road car-park which remains today.

There were woods we enjoyed. Some 45 acres of Franklands Wood went for Franklands Village in the mid 1930's, a time of great economic depression. Because of this, the newly formed local Rotary Club conceived the idea of both giving employment and providing much needed living accommodation. Forming a Housing Society, houses and flats were erected for reasonably priced rents — and Franklands Village was born. Wood Ride and Sunnywood Drive took small areas of woodland.

The first council owned houses were built in the mid 20's in New England Road, followed by those in both Mayflower and Woodlands Roads, after which the Bentswood estate was developed from Bents Wood. It was a lovely wood with its footpaths from New England Road and Oathall Road, where now is Oathall Avenue.

At the lower end of New England Road was a wide gate, at its side a small entrance for pedestrians, but to gain entry through the big one a key was needed, obtainable at the first cottage. Once acquired the opened gate led into a rural America Lane on the right hand side of which were single-storeyed, thatched cottages. Established in 1825 by William Allen, the Quaker philanthropist, each tenant had one acre of land, well-water, a cow, a pig and chicken, all at a minimal rent. Thus equipped, it was thought he could be self-supporting. Much later the cottages were connected to the main water supply, and the livestock ceased to be provided. I well recall going with my mother, to visit Miss Marchant, who with her brother, lived in one of these cottages, and as we were leaving, the old lady said to me, "Would you like a crack of nuts?". In the garden, lowered into the earth, was a large stone jar full of hazel nuts, which had grown on their land. I went home with the hazel nuts and the memory of an expression quite new to me — "a crack of nuts". The little thatched cottages, having fallen into a bad state of repair, were condemned under a demolition order of 1937, and toward the end of the last war, were replaced with much needed houses. Today, with a greater awareness for conservation, one is left to wonder if they might have been restored and saved. William Allen's name lives on in the name of Lindfield's William Allen Lane and our Allen Road; while Hanbury Lane, in the town, serves as a reminder of Allen's connection with the pharmaceutical firm, Allen and Hanbury.

We are taking a walk together through part of Haywards Heath, and later on we shall take another walk in a different section of the town, and each time we shall compare what is today with what was yesterday. We shall start at the Eight Arches on the border of this town with Burgess Hill, and to get there we'll board a bus. It's not a Southdown,

BENTS WOOD AND FOOTPATH TO LINDFIELD, HAYWARDS HEATH.   G.9385.

From here came the council owned housing estate.

At the lower end of New England Road, the gate lead to a rural America Lane

America Lane showing William Allen's thatched cottages.

for the company formed in 1915 with its familiar green and cream vehicles, is no more, but it served us well for many years. Before the last war, one old penny would take us, from the bus stop at the Sussex Hotel to the railway station; and from the same stop, a 'bus to Brighton would cost 2/6 return. If we chose to travel on the number 23, we could ride upstairs with an open top. In addition to the driver, there was a conductor, who punched us a ticket of stiff card — not paper as used today.

Here we are, at the Valebridge Viaduct, known to us as Eight Arches, so we dismount, and turning our backs on our neighbouring town, we walk under the arch. On the right hand side, a little gate is still here, it used to open on to a footpath which led over the field a short distance to Nos 1 and 2 Railway Cottages, Folly Hill. They were two houses near the line, built for railway employees, and I recall a visit to one of them, many years ago. The man of the house, Mr Foster, was on duty in the nearby Folly signal-box; and as we sat in the house a steam-train thundered past the window, alarming me, but Mrs Foster seemed not to notice being so used to it. Now those houses have gone, demolished in the 1970's.

We pass Folly Farm and go up Rookery Lane — never called by its correct name, for Rocky Lane it's always been and probably always will be. At the top end we come to what was known as Asylum Corner: on our left is Wivelsfield Road, on the right, Fox Hill, formerly Scrase Hill or Scrases Hill, but never to be confused with Scrase Bridge at the lower end of Oathall Road. Our way lies along Colwell Road; we knew it as Asylum Road, for here was the asylum, and the road at the rear, Hurstwood Lane, was Asylum Lane.

In 1859 on Hurst House Farm, the Sussex Lunatic Asylum was built. In my childhood it was the Brighton County Borough Asylum, and did not admit patients from this area, admission for us was to Hellingly. This was altered under the National Health Service Act in 1948, as was its name, to St Francis Hospital. Previously we had known next to nothing about this hospital, in fact by the majority of the general public, mental health had been misunderstood, and psychiatry itself was, to a large extent, a matter of custodial care. Gates were kept locked, and this mental hospital, in common with others, was a self-supporting village behind its walls. Today there is such a difference in psychiatry, and we have patients living within our community. Thankfully there has come a better understanding of mental illness, by the public, though we have a long way to go.

One of the hospital's landmarks was the 120' boiler-house chimney, taken down at the end of 1975. Another, still there today, is the water-tower. The hospital is now no more, its doors shut and locked on the 17th November 1995. However, the building is a listed one, and 1998 saw, going on the market, the first phase of residential development, Southdowns Park. Although knowing little about the hospital in earlier days, there was a sense of sadness felt at its closure, for in later years it had become very much a part of Haywards Heath, its open days and annual summer fair contributing to this. Perhaps, one day, a complete history will be written and it would certainly make interesting reading.

We must continue our walk, so leaving Colwell Road, we walk down on the right-hand side of Franklynn Road. Across the other side we see semidetached houses built in 1935 by Thomas White as part of the Haute Terre estate, and priced then at £650. Older property was obtainable at a lower figure, but these were modern and of course, contained a bathroom. The soil of Sussex containing suitable material for the making of bricks, it is understandable that the county contained many brick-fields, and Haywards Heath had its share. Builders would make their own bricks — Jesse Finch, a local builder, owned one on the south side of College Road, and another here, where we are standing, and upon it was built in 1935, Dellney Avenue by Arthur Langridge. With its building, went a little old thatched cottage, originally on Petlands farm, but later the home of William Botting, who had the

Asylum Corner, the junction of Rocky Lane, Wivelsfield and Colwell Roads with Fox Hill. The latter then was Scrase Hill, & Colwell Rd was Asylum Rd.

Aerial view of St.Francis Hospital.

nickname, "Fiddle", and his cottage, to the local people, was always "Fiddle" Botting's Cottage.

We walk a little further, and see blocks of flats on the opposite side, which took the place of Thomas White's builder's yard, and his brickfield was in Western Road. Long after houses were built upon it, the conductors of the No. 84 town 'bus, would continue to announce the 'bus stop there, as "Brickfield". The cemetery is at the bottom of the Western Road hill, consecrated in 1917 by the then Bishop of Chichester. It was certainly needed, for the St Wilfrid's graveyard, previously extended, was fast filling up, burial, not cremation, was the norm.

We walk on, passing Franklynn Court, built upon Berry's coal-yard. Opposite, on the Triangle Road corner, there stood for very many years, a bakery and a baker's shop; now we see sheltered accommodation. On the top of its octagonal turret, stands a weather vane, the work of Ben Autie, a Lewes blacksmith, showing a baker with a long coat and floppy hat, offering a tray of bread rolls — a fitting tribute to what was there.

We have now arrived at the Priory Restaurant. The history of the Priory of Our Lady of Good Counsel, began in 1886 when a group of nuns, with their chaplain, arrived at Hazelgrove Park, from Bruges, and started a girls' boarding-school. The foundation stone of the Priory Chapel was laid in 1890, and opened a year later. The grounds were extensive, and for necessity many buildings were erected. Until the 1960's the order was an enclosed one, it was also at that time that, with reluctance, the school finished. The Priory doors were closed in 1977, and a year later, came the move out of the town. House building on the land had already started, with the first residents arriving in 1972 to what became known as the Priory Estate. The Priory itself became a listed building. We remember Sister Anne Augustine in her wheel-chair, being pushed by Sister Mary Gertrude, always accompanied by Puck, their

Jack Russell terrier, for they became well known characters, and Keith Hilton, a local artist, put them on to a snow-scene canvas. Their move from the town, took them to a newly-built monastery at Sayers Common.

The car-park on the other side of the road next to the Sussex Hotel, was once home to greenhouses owned by Grimsdick and Son, nurserymen of Sussex Square. When we look at shops in the town, we will meet them again, but for now, our walk is finished: another day — another walk.

Grimsdick's Nursery, now car park, Franklynn Road

CHAPTER 6

WIDE-EYED WITH WONDER

"Saw the Vision of the world, and all the wonder that would be"
Alfred Tennyson

It would not be possible for young people today, to realise our enormous sense of wonder, when the wireless came into our homes. First a wireless-pole was erected at the far end of the rear garden, which, despite its name, supported a long wire aerial, then came the crystal set and two pair of earphones. The set, a black box some 7"x 5" contained tuning coils, a crystal and a small finely coiled piece of wire called a 'cat's whisker'. Reception was obtained by tuning the coils and resting the end of the 'cat's whisker' on various parts of the crystal until a station was 'detected' but when obtained, the sheer wonder was enormous. Several attempts may have been necessary for success and the vibrations from a horse and cart passing the house could dislodge it, and we would need to find that right spot on the crystal, once again. A near neighbour 'listening in' — as it was called — shouted excitedly to his wife, "I can hear Big Ben — Big Ben from London". My father's reaction was of a more quiet reverence, as he remarked, "Well, it causes one to wonder what is in the ether."

I was allowed to 'listen in' to Children's Hour, which actually wasn't quite an hour. The presenters were known as 'aunties' and 'uncles', except one, who was J.K. and J.K. became ill. Then came day when we were told that he was dead: it was my first brush with death, and in some strange childlike way, I mourned the passing of a man I never knew. For a shilling, which was donated to a Sunshine Home for Blind Babies, there would be a mention of a birthday, and directions to where a present would be found. With my party in progress, my mother implored me to put on the earphones in case my birthday was mentioned — and it was. I was to follow the strings from the piano, and found they led me up the stairs and down again and back to the piano, where, on the floor, was a gift, which hadn't been there a couple of minutes earlier. The contents of that present, have long gone from memory, but the excitement of a mention on the wireless, was to last a considerable time. What it is to be young, for the acceptance of one of my poems on television a few years ago, could leave me quite unmoved.

'Uncle Mac' would be in the studio, if the birthday was for twins, and he would say, in a resonant voice, "Hello twins": and when he was there, it would fall to him to say the "Goodnight", and always he would say, "Goodnight children. Be good, — but not so good, that someone says, 'Now I wonder what he's up to' ".War time, and children evacuated, the goodnight was always, "Goodnight children — everywhere".

The crystal set was to be replaced, with one made by my elder brother, which was a much improved version in a wooden case, being electrically powered with valves and a loudspeaker and with better performance and no earphones needed. Of course, familiarity breeding contempt, we were becoming a little more blasé. These early sets needed accumulators for storing the electrical energy, and for these my father made two wooden boxes, each with a wide leather strap as a handle. It was my job on a Saturday to take one needing to be charged, to Mr James' electrical shop in South Road and to bring home the fully charged one, left with him the previous week.

My father, being a violinist, meant there had always been music within the home as long as I can remember, but the advent of a wireless and my brother Leslie's gramophone, widened our musical horizons. The first one he had, was a small affair encased in tin, and needing very small records — not much more than a toy; but a later one was a real beauty, and certainly gave us a great appreciation of classical music, which remains with me.

It was quite usual to see children, carrying their music-cases, trotting along to their teacher for a lesson. Three lived very near to us, the brass plate on the wall of 29, Haywards Road, proclaimed to all, that here lived Miss Towner, L.R.A.M. A.T.C.L.. No such qualifications for Miss Hatton, but many were the pupils accepted for piano lessons at 5, Gower Road; but it was to number 79 in the same road that I went at nine years of age, to Miss Button, a retired school teacher. I have never ceased to be grateful to my parents for those lessons, for piano playing is still today one of my greatest pleasures. I had the promise from my father, that school homework behind me, he would teach me to play the violin, but it was not to be, for while I was still at school, he died.

The wireless, gramophone and piano, all gave pleasure, but films too were another source of enjoyment, and although, as a family, we weren't great cinema-goers, many were. The Heath Theatre, under its gabled roof in the Broadway, had opened in 1911, and, until films with sound came about, it had shown silent films with captions. The 'talkies', as they became known, were thought to be wonderful. The Heath Theatre closed in 1932, and by 1937 the building was being totally redesigned for gas-showrooms, with the loss of the gabled roof for a flat one, but the gain of Mr Therm, the logo of the gas-board for many years. He pirouetted on one foot from the top of the building, and we miss him, now that shops occupy the site. Early cinemas were known as picture-palaces.

The reason for the closure of our first cinema, was the opening of the Broadway Cinema, quite near the other, at the top of Perrymount Road. It backed on to the railway line, with its frontage back from the road, and steps leading down to its foyer. It served well from 1932 until its closure in 1954, when a little later it became the furnishing showrooms of the local firm of J.W.Upton and Son. Its life ended in 1987, when it was demolished for an office block.

In 1933 we heard that there was to be a new cinema built in Perrymount Road. It was to have the latest projection system, which would give the screen a 'stereoscopic' effect; the stage was to be designed for variety turns; and with the cinema there was to be a dance-hall and a restaurant. A prize was to be offered for guessing its name. On Saturday, 30th.May 1936 the Perrymount Cinema opened on a site near Commercial Square. Following the second world war, the television was to hit the cinemas, and attendances fell, and despite local opposition and a petition of over 1,000 signatures, our one remaining cinema was closed in November 1972. It was demolished in 1984 for offices.

About the time that wireless was entering our homes, something new and exciting was to be seen in the sky — aeroplanes. Local postcard collectors may well be familiar with such names as Oscar Morison, P.Howard Pixton and E.C.Gordon England, some of the pioneer aviators, their flimsy aircraft often coming to grief, especially with their endeavouring to land in Oakwood Road at Oakwood — now demolished, but then the family home of Mr England. The year was 1911, but during the four year period of the Great War, restrictions were placed upon civil aviation, and it was not until 1919 that they were lifted. So when I was young, it was not a common sight to see an aeroplane and one heard approaching, would bring people out-of-doors, to gaze skywards.

I remember being told of clerical workers at the Boltro Road post-office, hearing the approach of a plane, running from their office at the rear of the building to the front, where they stood on the pavement, gazing up at this unusual sight. Mr Percy Hall was the first to find his voice, excitement and awe causing a stutter, as he said, "A-and there are p-people up there, aren't there?"

Our Council School headmaster Mr Owen Freestone, had two sons, the younger, John, was to become well known in both scholastic and musical circles. 'Dick', the elder, trained as a pilot, starting his career as a cadet at Cranford, going on to Tangmere, and ultimately becoming an Air-Commodore. One day, long before that, Mr Freestone announced to the school, that his pilot son was to fly over the school that afternoon at a certain time, and we were to be allowed out into the playground to watch. An air of excitement pervaded as we all trooped out, and then, right on time, the plane roared in, circled, looped the loop, swooped down low over us, and was gone, but not before the whole school had waved its thanks to the pilot. We were left <u>most</u> impressed, and <u>very</u> proud that the pilot was the son of our headmaster.

Air travel now is taken for granted, and the Gatwick Airport seen today, bears no resemblance to the one I visited during the last war.

Flying at Oakwood, Haywards Heath, 7 & 8 May 1911

The flimsy structure shown here of an early plane.

CHAPTER 7

CHURCHES

"Come all to church, good people" A.E.Housman

Positioned near the centre of the county, standing on high ground, and floodlit at night, is the church of St Wilfrid, our parish church: in my time it has always been there, but it wasn't always so. In 1856 services were being held in the loft of a carpenter's shop, where part of Great Heathmead now stands. Later, when a very small St. Wilfrid's School was built at the bottom corner of Church Road, services were conducted there. The population of some 400 was on the increase, and a permanent building was becoming a necessity, and part of the Haywards Heath Inclosure was awarded by the Commissioners for that purpose. In 1863, on St Wilfrid's Day, the cornerstone was laid. Two years later services were being held, though the church had no clock, and only a very small graveyard. It was then that the ecclesiastical parish was taken out of Cuckfield, becoming a separate one. The graveyard was extended in 1888; and the clock in the tower that Lord Leconfield set in motion on Empire Day in 1921, was the town peace memorial.

In 1997 the interior of the church was given a new look, and in the following year, a new pipe organ was installed. Much could be written about the entire project, but the end result needs to be seen — and it can be, for the church doors are open daily, to all.

To serve the residents in the northern end of the town, the Chapel of the Holy Spirit was erected in 1897. An iron building, it stood on a corner plot of Sydney Road and what was to become Church Avenue. It was originally in the same ecclesiastical parish as St Wilfrid's Church, becoming a separate one in 1916 with it's name altered to St Richard's church. Always present was a vision of a more permanent building, and this came about in 1938, when the church we see today was ready for worship. Later a hall was erected at the rear, and the former iron building, which had been used as a hall, was demolished, making way for houses.

I can remember the iron Church of the Ascension in the Asylum Twitten (St John's Road), although it was, by then, no longer in use. It had been built in 1895 to serve that area, but the moving of the Congregationalists in 1915 to South Road, left a vacated building in Wivelsfield Road which became St Edmund's Church for Anglican use. The 1950's saw rapid development in the Sheppey's area, and 1966 saw the closure of the Wivelsfield Road church and the opening of one in Vale Road, and the naming of it was a happy link with that former little iron church — The Church of the Ascension. The vacated church in Wivelsfield Road became the Kingdom Hall for the Jehovah's Witnesses in 1970 until their move to Burgess Hill in the 1990's. The building remains as a hall.

In New England Road is the Church of the Presentation of Christ in the Temple. That is the name in full, but it is usual to hear, or read of it, as the Presentation Church. It was another iron church, opened in 1882, and served till 1897, when it became a Sunday School and parish room, for a new brick-built church. Fire destroyed the original building in 1979, and today a new hall stands in its place.

The Evangelical Free Church in the same road was built in 1967, replacing an earlier one of 1936, which became the church hall.

Franklands Village has its own church in the Church of the Good Shepherd, which superseded the Upper Room, its earlier venue which was also in the village.

Sussex Road has two churches, one on the hill, near the Petlands Road entrance, is Jireh Chapel, a Strict Baptist Church, which has stood there since 1879, and has its own burial ground.

A different kind of Baptist worship is conducted in a church a little further along the road. Previously worshipping in the Albermarle Centre, the move to Sussex Road was made in the spring of 1994.

The church to which they moved had been built for, and used by, the Primitive Methodists, being built in 1877. In the 1950's, both the interior and the exterior were redesigned, but it closed in 1991.

The Wesleyan Methodist Church was in Perrymount Road. The Primitive and Wesleyan Methodists uniting at national level in 1932, we now know the local church simply as the Haywards Heath Methodist Church. Prior to its opening in 1900, worship was in a room at Mr Whall's shop in Boltro Road. For use as a Sunday School and hall, an iron building was erected in 1912, and it was not until 1959 that it was replaced by the Wesley Hall built by Mr A.H.Langridge. 1983 saw it being extended.

Christian Scientists, or to give them their correct title, The First Church of Christ, Scientist, moved from Fir Tree End, in Church Road, to the remaining part of the former St Wilfrid's School, on the corner of Church and South Roads, in 1956, and their Reading Room is there.

The Congregational Church, having moved from Wivelsfield Road to South Road in 1915, being built by a local builder Mr Thomas White, was therefore new when I was taken there at the age of three. Its hall stood at the rear, an army post office from the 1914-1918 war. It served well until 1959, when Mr W.C.Hilton built a single storey brick hall, a further two storeys being added by Stephen Knight and Co; from Cuckfield, and opened in 1967. The church stands there today as the

United Reformed Church, which evolved from a national level merge of Congregationalists and Presbyterians in England.

Roman Catholics in this area were worshipping in the south transept of the Priory Chapel, till a piece of ground was donated by the nuns of the Priory for the building of a church, in Hazelgrove Road. The Church of St Paul was built and opened with a special Mass on the 12th June 1930. The doors of this beautiful church are open to all, daily.

These are some of our churches — buildings; but Churches are people, and it was those people early on, who recognized a lack of social life within the town, and met that need with children's clubs, youth guilds, women's meetings, men's clubs and much more.

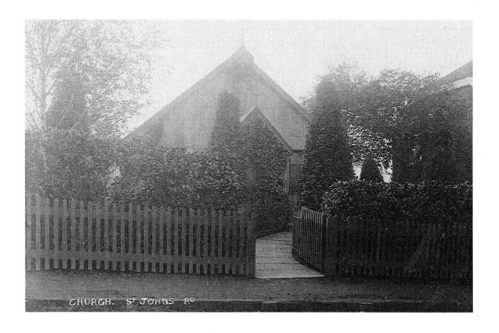

The Church of the Ascension, St John's Road.
Opened 1895

CHAPTER 8

SQUEAKY-CLEAN

"Let all things be done decently and in order"   1 Corinthians 14. 40

"Keep it. It might come in useful one day", was a well-worn saying from my mother. Had she been married to a millionaire, I really believe she would have been exactly the same, for she hated waste. Never did we have fire-wood for the kitchener, newspaper was rolled, twisted and deftly knotted, and that laid, with the coal on top, would get the fire going. There had to be no cutting of the string, however impatient to open a parcel, knots had to be unpicked, the string was to be re-used. Paper bags were kept, so was wrapping paper, and Christmas paper treated with care for re-use. No buying of soap-flakes, from the bar of washing soap, flakes were made from a large-holed food-grater kept specifically for that purpose. Several pairs of black boots or shoes within the home would merit the purchase of shoe polish, but the one pair of brown shoes of mine, as a child, were cleaned with the inner side of a banana skin. Why buy brown polish for one pair of shoes for a fast-growing child? Why indeed? Thinking that little economy was peculiar to my mother, when grown up, I enquired of others, to find it was fairly normal. Always kept handy in the scullery was a card of pot-menders, metal discs, for prolonging the life of an aluminium saucepan with a hole in its base.

Felt insoles for shoes were cut from the brims of old hats, finger-stalls from old kid gloves. I have still a mental vision of my mother returning home on a Saturday with her shopping, and unwrapping the rashers of bacon. First the white kitchen paper was removed, laid flat upon the table and smoothed, then folded in two and torn into two halves, one given to Leslie, one to me. When at fourteen he went to work, the whole piece was mine. That kitchen paper was our drawing book. Underneath was grease-proof paper, this would be wiped clean and used for covering the top of a steamed pudding. Any white material was boiled and kept clean for bandages, while coloured material, small pieces left from dressmaking, found their way into a ragbag, and were kept for patching. Material at that time was either cotton or wool, there was no-man made fibre. The school curriculum included knitting, needlework, patching, darning and housewifery — we were to be good housewives.

For the housewife there were particular days for individual jobs, and Monday was washday — but no washing machine, no spin-drier, no tumble-dryer. First the copper had to be filled with water, and the fire lit beneath it; then came a soaking of all cotton garments, coloureds and whites being kept separate, after which they would be washed, in water that had to be heated, and after a rinsing, the whites were transferred to the copper. The coloureds had a rinse, sometimes two, and the same for the whites, removed from the copper with a copper-stick, after their boiling. To wring the water from them all, the mangle wheel was turned and the clothes fed into the wooden rollers. Now all could go on the garden clothes -line, but not before starch was used for some articles— starch that needed to be made with boiling water, and for the white garments, in the last rinse, a Reckitt's blue-bag needed to be used, for a whiter than white finish. Finally the copper could be emptied and the clearing up done. Tomorrow was another day, when the flat-irons would be heated on the kitchener and the ironing and the airing would be done. Throughout the week there was always, for the housewife, the making, the mending, the patching, the darning of socks and stockings.

Bedrooms were cleaned on Fridays, the downstairs cleaning on Saturdays. The flue of the kitchener was swept, blacklead applied to the stove, and polished till it shone; brass was cleaned, the hearth and front doorstep whitened with hearthstone, floors were washed. I had to make myself scarce, while Leslie, with the cutlery, resorted to the shed. It was his task to clean it, and I counted myself most fortunate that stainless cutlery came into the home, before that job would have come my way. There was, however, a bright spot during the morning, for it was pocket-money day and I would be given 1d. —one penny. One halfpenny could be spent, the other saved in my money-box, for thrift had to be encouraged.

Saturday night was bath-night, when the long galvanized bath would be put down before the kitchener and filled. The red afternoon table-cloth was pulled low, to exclude draughts, and while my non-smoking father went out to buy his sweets, my mother bathed and hair-washed Leslie and I, until we were old enough not to need her. I was ten before the type of bath we know today, came into the home. After Saturday, the house and its occupants were clean and ready for the next day — Sunday.

Sunday, then, was a holy day, as against the holiday it has become today, for so many. For my father, a life-deacon, and choir-member at the Congregational Church, it meant church attendance at both morning and evening services, for me it was Sunday School and church. In those days it was usual to sit quietly, without talking, before the start of the service, in preparation for worship, but today we seem to have lost that reverence in most places of worship. It's a pity. Quite purposely my mother made Sunday somewhat different within the home. Instead of the usual coloured table-cloth, there was always a starched white one to grace the table, for the roast dinner and again at teatime. The best china was used, and instead of the usual water to drink at dinner time, there was lemonade, made at home, with real lemons, and served in a cut-glass jug. We also dressed differently on Sunday wearing our best clothes.

In the town there was a very occasional shop open, for sweets or cigarettes, on a Sunday; no evening trading, or Bank Holidays; and a weekly half-day closure which, in this town, was on a Wednesday. Of course, there were people who had to work on a Sunday, but by and large, it was a quiet day of rest — and a holy day.

It might be supposed that with all the systematic cleaning done within the home, no other was necessary, but those were days of open fires and chimneys that needed to be swept, so yearly, at the end of winter, came the Spring clean. Evidently it was not during that time that John Howard Payne wrote------"Be it ever so humble, there's no place like home", for those not involved tried to keep out of the way. First of all the sweep needed to be booked, and booked well in advance, for he was a man in great demand. No vacuum cleaning, he came with rods and brushes, and up the chimney they went and down came the soot. Then the Spring cleaning commenced.

Wardrobes, cupboards, turned out, drawers re-lined, paint-work washed, curtains washed, starched and pegged on the line, blinds removed from the windows and cleaned, carpets on the clothes-line were hit with a hand carpet-beater, china ornaments dusted throughout the year, were washed in soapy water. Nothing escaped the attention of the housewife, until the whole house was clean, and then for many, no fire would be lit until the next winter, however cold the Spring weather might become. My mother would have none of that, and should colder days follow the Spring clean, she would say, "We can't be cold", and light the fire. One Gower Road couple became so cold one evening they went for a walk to get warm, and seeing smoke from our chimney, the shivering husband said to his wife, "Well, there's <u>one</u> wise woman".

Normal service could be resumed after that yearly event, and all heaved a sigh of relief.

CHAPTER 9

ANOTHER WALK

"I will----talk with you, walk with you."   William Shakespeare

Another walk - and this time we'll start at the shop that is now the Picturesque Gallery, on the corner of Triangle and Sussex Roads and walk to the top of Wivelsfield Road , and down again on the other side. Our starting point was once Waterloo House, and it was here that James Box had his butcher's shop and adjoining it, a grocery, so it seemed quite logical to call the hill sloping down by his shops, Box's Hill. The Mid-Sussex Directory and Visitors' Guide published periodically by Charles Clarke Ltd; told us it was a continuation of Sussex Road, but it was to us <u>always</u> Box's Hill. The corner we see today, came about in 1986 when Waterloo House was demolished, and it was then that an old well was discovered. Unfortunately it was found impossible to make it a feature of the new development, but the terra-cotta Tudor roses that graced the old building were retained, and incorporated into the present one, and can be seen in the front wall.

On we go, down the hill, and the shop, Newcroft, was Mrs Green's general shop, while Mr Green was a coal, coke and wood merchant. We come to a hall, that was built for a Congregational Church and ready for worship in 1861, closing in 1915, with its move to South Road. The empty building was used as a furniture store by Ernest Miller, till once again it became a church, St Edmunds, and that is how I remember it. It was at a service in that first Congregational church, that my parents met for the first time.

On we go, and here's the public house, The Wivelsfield, but it was The New Inn at first when I knew it, until with modernisation and a face-lift, it became the Ugly Duckling. Rock Cottages have been demolished, but the shop was here, and I can remember being sat in the pushchair and brought to the shop, when Mr Upton had it for furniture. We shall come to his business again in the Broadway and Perrymount Road.

It was where we stand now, that in a house named Kentville, Mr Gater ran a sub-post-office. Now we have come to a little road, linking Wivelsfield Road to Colwell Road. It had, and still has, no name, but to us it was always Checker's Hill — or should it have been Chequer's? Now we will cross the road, walking back toward the top of our old Box's Hill again.

There were no bungalows nor houses at the top of this side of the road, except, of course, the two old houses, which are here today, Old Nursery and Big Pennys. No Edward Road, but where we see Dinnages forecourt there were three cottages, Little Pennys, and nearby there was once a forge, and later a stonemason worked there. The United Services Club was built and opened in 1973 to replace former premises in Perrymount Road; and where we are now there was a brook, so maybe the houses we see opposite, Spring Gardens, had a water connection rather than the time of year. Up Box's Hill we go, and on the top corner, Miss Piper had a little draper's shop, on the door of which was a bell that jingle-jangled when the door was opened and closed.

Because that was a short walk, we'll take another this time starting from the top end of Perrymount Road. Here is Capital House, part of which was built where once stood the United Services Club, an iron building erected by ex-servicemen in 1922. It was replaced in 1973 by the one in Wivelsfield Road that we saw previously. Next to it was the Broadway Cinema, which after its closure in 1954, was altered to become house furniture showrooms for the firm J.W.Upton and Sons, their distinctive removal vans being well known in the district. The showrooms closed in 1987 to make way for the office-block we see today, and for the same reason, went a car showroom, shops, and two houses, Westover and The Nutshell. The early 1980's saw much office development in this road, so that house names, San Remo, St Hilda, Pontresina, Heathfield, Shortfield, Oakfield, Oakfield Terrace, Peartree, Clifton Gardens, Floretta and Oak Villa are but now memories. Between Pontresina and Heathfield, there was a neglected little Hudson Road, intended, once upon a time, to link with Boltro Road, but was never finished. It housed a hut used by the trades council.

Here we are at Clair Road, and near the bottom end were some railway cottages that led from it, Clair Place, but they were both renamed in 1933 after the electrification of the railway. Previously they were Station Road and Station Place, and at the end of the road was the down entrance to the station. There were then no platform tickets, and for pedestrians in Perrymount Road needing Boltro Road, the station subway was not only a short cut, but a free one. Although standing empty for six years, it was as recent as 1997 that the Liverpool Arms was demolished. Early in its life it had been enlarged, and a brick in part of that enlargement bore the letters L.B.S.C. As the London, Brighton and South Coast Railway came from amalgamation of the London Brighton Railway and the South Coast Railway, and that was in 1846, we have a little idea of the date of enlargement.

Up Clair Road and into Perrymount again, and before the end, there were houses, then right on the corner were Finch's builders workshops which stood empty for some time, before being demolished for a 'bus station which opened in 1954 – to close in 1980.

We'll cross the road and walk along that side. A short way up, stood a private residence – St Clair, a lodge standing at the front end of its drive, its grounds, on the lower side, extending around into Sydney Road, and on the upper side to the recreation ground entrance. The 1930's brought the shops we see today, sweeping around into Sydney Road, and the Perrymount Cinema, with dance-hall, café-restaurant and shops incorporated with it, built in 1936. The lodge, altered, became in 1932,

St Clair, Perrymount Road: Commercial Road end.

St Clair Cottage

Finch's workshops, Commercial Square end of Perrymount Road, demolished 1954 for bus station.

offices for the estate agents, Bradley and Vaughan; and the house itself became a school from 1935-1969, before being demolished in 1973. St Clair meadow, on the upper side, stood behind tall, green, iron railings, but in 1935, being by then council owned, was opened up as a children's playground. Mrs Stride, the then council chairman, cut the white ribbon suspended across the steps of the slide, and the several hundred children watching, shouted with glee, as she, and other council members, mounted the steps, and shot down that slide. A bouquet was presented to Mrs Stride by little Pamela Whatford. It remained a play area until the building of Clair Hall in 1974.

We have reached one of several entrances to the 'rec'. Although not a native of the town, my mother had acquired quite a store of local history before I came along, and she would share this with me on our walks. About the 'rec' she would tell me how it was originally a surviving piece of what the town we know today was like years ago; and how it was purchased by public subscription in 1887, as a memorial to Queen Victoria's Golden Jubilee. The cricket area had been the brain child of Mr Jesse Finch, to clear that area from discarded rubbish and drain it. It was officially opened ten years later, in Queen Victoria's Diamond Jubilee year of 1897. The pavilion came three years later, and the latter, as well as the cricket-ground, was opened by Mr T.Bannister, the council's chairman at the time. Mr Jesse Finch was one of the principal builders in the Mid-Sussex district, and served the town in local government, as did Mr Thomas White, another well known builder. What my mother didn't tell me, Mr Finch's obituary has — he had left the little Horsted Keynes school at nine years old, and started work for a few pence a day.

Not far from the rec' entrance was a baker's shop, one of three Mr Snell had in the town. Here is the Methodist church, Wesleyan till 1932, and no Wesley Hall next to it, but tennis-courts at one time. Houses there were, their names now but memories, names like Heathdene, Isenhurst, Barbers; but two house names live on in blocks of flats, Jireh and Ormerod, for just as offices replaced dwelling-houses on the opposite side of the road, so have flats on this side.

Up the hill we go, the path some height from the road, the bank below the path, was a grassy one with trees, until the latter were removed, and the bank was faced with the crazy paving we see today. It was a Sussex Road, jobbing builder, Mr Stephen Brooker, who carried out that work, and would seem to have done it very well.

Here we are at the top of the hill, and our walk is finished.

Perrymount Road.

CHAPTER 10

SHOPS

"Are you being served?"   B.B.C.1 Series

We were indeed served, for there was no self-service, no supermarkets, yet alone hypermarkets. Individual shopkeepers kept to their own trade, if we wanted meat we went to the butcher's, a grocer supplied our groceries, and our fish came from a fishmonger, and so on. Each shop had a polished counter, behind which stood the sales-assistant, and the customer would be met with, "Yes please?" or "Can I help you?" or in a busy shop, perhaps with more than one shop-assistant, the question might have been "Are you being served?" Good salesmanship was an art. Commercial Square – a Square then with no roundabout – had its own shops, following on from the Burrell Arms was a fishmonger, a butcher and a general shop. On the other side of the Square, at the beginning of Sydney Road, stood Beeny's Emporium, having moved from the top of Millgreen Road in 1893. The emporium stocked a very wide variety of goods, all under one roof, but in different departments.

Up Perrymount Road and into the Broadway, there were no lock-up shops on the left-hand side and the frontage from the corner of Heath Road presented a very rural appearance until Arnolds Cottage and Caffyns Garage were reached.

The garage, demolished in 1985, left the site for the Chelsea Parade we see today. From Wivelsfield Road, Mr Upton had transferred his furnishing business next to Caffyns in 1923, staying there till moving to the Broadway Cinema site in 1954. Next came a cycle shop, which I only just remember, I think it was Hampton's, and later the premises were used by the local Electric Supply Company, which became Central

Sussex Electricity Ltd. and later still Seeboard had their showrooms here. The whole block of that Dutch-gabled building, which extended around the corner into Church Road, was Coventry Building.

Had we walked up on the opposite side of the Broadway, we would have seen Mr Miller's furniture shop – later enlarged and we could have purchased grocery, wines and spirits, drapery, jewellery, cigarettes, shoes and dairy produce.

The last shop before the road over the tunnel was Broadley's a gentlemen's outfitters, established in 1896, staying till 1993. It was also the shop that made the nine year old girl I was, feel a millionaire. Walking by one morning, I was asked to go in, as they were making a coat for a girl about my size and wishing to save her two visits for fittings, as she lived quite a distance away, I was asked if I would have a fitting that day, and come again the next week. I complied, and was paid one shilling, — one whole shilling, never had such wealth come my way! Of course it had to be saved. Next to the shop stood Ardlin, a double-fronted house with hollyhocks in its garden. It was one time the home of Dr Newth, but I remember it as housing the dental practices of Cahill and Morgan. It was sold in 1937, a year later becoming the offices for the Haywards Heath Building Society until their move to South Road in 1989.

On the forecourts of the jewellers and the cigar stores, there were wooden racks for bicycles, and during the summer months, a drinking bowl for dogs was placed outside one shop.

Beeny's Emporium, Commercial Square, built 1893 an enlargement from former Millgreen Road premises.

Caffyn's Garage in the Broadway demolished 1985 for Chelsea Parade.

The Broadway.

The Broadway, Clifton Villas on the left, Church Rd on the right.

Broadway Chambers skirts the bend from where Ardlin was, around into the road over the tunnel, and the shops there are newer, supplying our need for bread, cakes, cigarettes, ladies' wear, and here was the showroom for the Haywards Heath and district Gas Company.

We cross the road that goes over the tunnel and there was a chemist, Dixon, so this area was always known by its unofficial name, Dixon's Corner, in fact it's still referred to as that by any who have lived here a long time. Once upon a time the shop had been a house, Clifton House, and this part of the Broadway was remembered even by my sister and brother, as Clifton Place, with Clifton Terrace and Clifton Villas near the public house, some of the latter I remember. Next to the chemist was Flinn and Son Ltd. the dyers and cleaners, then a stationer's kept by Miss Muzzell. A hazy memory gives me a remembrance of Hughes, a furniture shop, and of wool being sold by Mrs Vincent. To buy sweets, tobacco or newspapers in the shop next to the Star, we needed to mount a small flight of steps.

One of those Clifton Villas stands clearly in my memory, for one very hot afternoon I saw a car draw up. A car wasn't usual, and this one was being driven by a uniformed chauffeur who jumped out and opened the car door for his lady employer. The lady, having mounted the villa steps, was admitted into the house and the chauffeur waited. The sun was hot, his uniform was hot, so what a good idea to nip quickly up the steps of the sweet-shop and buy himself an ice-cream. No halfpenny cornet was this one, such as I might have had from Mr Faccenda's van when he came from Burgess Hill on a Saturday. This was a tuppenny wafer, but as it neared the lips of the chauffeur, the villa door opened, and the lady emerged. The ice-cream wafer was flung to the ground, as he hastened to open the car door. That tuppeny discarded wafer was lovely: well I couldn't leave it there to be wasted could I? I wonder if the lady had made the journey to book a nurse. I don't know, but two certainly lived there, Nurse Meadows and Nurse Brinkhurst, and a plate on the house wall, proclaimed they were Queen's Nurses.

In the late 1960's the increase of traffic within this area, was becoming dangerous, necessitating the closure of the road Muster Green North, the construction of Dolphin Road, and the introduction of a gyratory system.

From the National Westminster Bank to where Muster Court stands today, was part of Clevelands' garden, the house itself standing where the flats now are. The other side of what is now 'Nat West' was Mr Pratt's butchers shop, one of two he had, the other being in Sussex Road. Next to his shop were houses, then Cobb's Stores, a grocery, with a sub-post-office in one shop, the other a draper's, and from where the bank now stands to Cobb's Stores was once known as Stanford Place. On the opposite side of the road, was St Wilfrid's School, no Park Parade then, but the steps were there, leading to the footpath into Church Road. We called it Tar Path, and next to it, the churchyard. There were no more shops, for some third of a mile, only a house Brent Eleigh standing in its grounds, a County School and a Council School, till we met up again with shops.

Looking at the opposite side of the road, we should have seen only one shop after Cobb's Stores, and that was on the corner of Haywards Road. Our present parish magazine, "Ahead", gives an occasional glimpse into the archives of St Wilfrid's Church, making for most interesting reading. In 1895 we see the children of both day school and Sunday School being given a treat and – and here I quote, – "they marched to the large field below the church, which was kindly lent for the occasion by Mr Pannett." That "large field" is our Victoria Park. Incidentally, what a mammoth task that must have been for those in charge, for there were between 600 and 650 children.

Cobb's Stores on upper end of park, in one-time Stanford Place

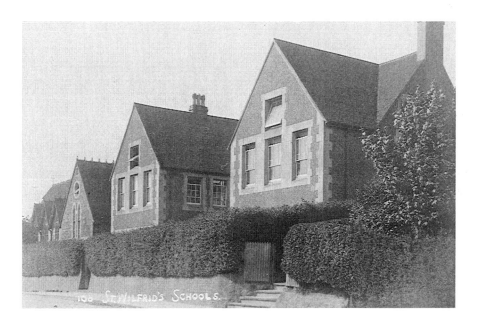

Northern end of South Rd, opposite the park; site now Park Parade.

The shops, Victoria Gate, next to the park, now stand where once we saw the fire station. A move to Millgreen Road left it empty in 1961, but it was not demolished until 1981. To the top of the hill there were houses, a few of their names still remembered, St Dorothy, St Hilda, Edelwiess. With its door right on the corner of South and Haywards Roads stood Mr Brenchley's grocer's shop, but houses demolished at the top of the hill, and shops replacing them, meant a move later on for his shop around the corner into South Road. Any grocer's shop had a lovely smell of its own – a combination of smells from coffee, cheese, bacon, in fact from all that was sold there. It is lost today, with the pre-wrapping of the supermarket.

There were two ways, for me, of going to school, either via Haywards Road, or through the twitten to South Road and the latter was, by far, the better, for having crossed South Road Miss Robinson's shop had to be passed. Not that we passed it without stopping to look in the window, for Miss Robinson had a toy shop, and it was only the first ringing of the school-bell, telling us to hurry, or the second ringing, when we knew we ought to be there and getting into lines, that would make us pass her shop without pausing. It stood on part of what today is Milward's shoe shop, and was well established by the time I knew it, for it finds a place in the 1902 directory. Her assistant for many years was Miss Margetts, and they were two gentle, patient souls.

We flattened our noses against the window, to feast our eyes on dolls, balls, guns, paints, crayons, pens, pencils, skipping-ropes, windmills, marbles, glass allies, fireworks, coloured matches, sparklers, masks, spinning and humming tops, wooden hoops for girls, iron hoops and skids for the boys. That was half of the window display, the other part was given to uninteresting things that grown up people bought, like stationery and fancy goods; and they also went into the shop, for the lending library. What an Aladdin's Cave it was to us. Miss Piper – the lady with the little draper's shop at the top end of Box's Hill – told me of a group of young male carol-singers, letting forth lustily at her door

Cottages on left were Pelham Cottages: in Pelham Place.

with "----peace on earth and mercy mild----". Giving them a copper or two, she enquired of how the money was going to be spent, to receive the ready reply, "We're going up Miss Robinson's to buy a gun with it." Miss Piper laughed at the irony.

'Our' toyshop closed in 1938, upon Miss Robinson's retirement. One year later, local men, who might well have bought, in childhood, their toy guns in her shop, were killing and being killed with the real thing. We remember that Aladdin's Cave with fondness. I wonder if out there — wherever that 'out there' might have been during the war — when thoughts turned to home, in a temporary calm between the hell of bitter fighting, would one of those thoughts have been of a particular little toyshop, somewhere in a peaceful England.

Back to South Road, and the Hazelgrove Road corner, where the shop, Grimsdick and Son, stood. They, too, were well established, for Mr E.Grimsdick had opened a small shop in Sussex Road in the early 1890's, as a nurseryman and seedsman. A little later he saw two houses being built in Sussex Square, one with its frontage on South Road, the other on Hazelgrove Road, and he realised that was the position he wanted, to enable his business to expand. So from the flat over his former shop, he moved into one large house, converted from the two already being constructed, named it Western House, and by 1895 was already trading from a shop at those premises, in Crossways – later Sussex Square. By the time I remember it, the shop had been altered, and in front of its door, on the corner, was an attractive, circular, little garden, and to the best of my knowledge, it was never vandalised. They had a nursery, where now there is a car-park at the lower end of Franklynn Road, and land in Ashenground Road, taken for houses. On that land was the foreman's house, Pury End, his son living in it today. Not that Mr Edwards was always foreman, he was but fourteen years old, when he left school and went there to work, and apart from war service in the Boer War, spent the whole of his working life there. Ashenground Road had two attractions for us, as children. On Pury End 'gold' letters advertised Grimsdick and Son, Nurseries, and we knew no other house bearing 'gold' letters; neither did we have any knowledge of another house, with a golden privet armchair on its front lawn, such as there was at one of Gladstone Villas.

Taking a leisurely stroll along a quiet South Road, tea could have been taken at Cruttenden's Café, and after refreshment, Mr Smith was in a shop nearby to fit us with footwear, and when the latter showed signs of wear, Mr Verrall's business would have repaired them. To visit Mr Banbury, or a little later Mr Tullett, would have needed an appointment, for they were photographers at the South Road Studio. Both Mr Gassett and Mr Stephenson would have sold us jewellery, and a good selection of hats was stocked by Ellena. There were houses, Pelham Terrace in Pelham Place, and a plot or two of land. Before the Council School was reached, Mr George Hilton was selling furniture, soft furnishing, and conducting funerals He had started business in 1882 at Acton House, Crossways (Sussex Square), and within my collection, a photograph shows Mr Hilton and a very young lad, standing outside of the shop. Might it not be probable that the boy represented the whole staff, and would have been responsible for deliveries on a hand-cart?

And now we cross the road, walking down from Haywards Road. My mother would tell me, that right on the corner was Mr Sherlock's garden, of the house in which he lived, Canton Cottage. He was a sea-faring man, and on that garden had built a pretty little model house, from the many sea-shells he had collected. It would have been quite an attraction; a cousin of mine once told me, how she would say to her sister, "Let's go and look at the pretty man's house" (*sic*). I saw no such wonder, for all that was left for me to view from the pushchair, was one blue wall. On that garden, Mrs Rainsford once had the Canton Café, and I recall, while at the Council School, seeing one of the boys, run from the school, across to the café at play time. Sweets were sold there, and I expect a ha'penny or a penny was burning a hole in his pocket. What he did was forbidden, and we girls watched holding our breaths, till his return. The Lloyds Bank we see there today, started life on the garden and was later extended to the site of demolished Canton Cottage.

Mr German had his dental practice in one of Gordon Villas, and next to houses were a few shops: Mrs Brown had a cycle store, and there I used to go to buy my brother's carbide, for his bicycle lamp. Water had to be put with it to produce acetylene gas, and the smell was horrible, but the white light it produced was worth the odour, for previous lights were from oil.

Mr Adams was in charge of the Singers Sewing Machine Company's shop, and a seed shop was there, where I went for linseed. Let one of us, in the home, become 'chesty', and my mother would go into action, producing linseed-tea. She flavoured it with liquorice – not the type we children bought for a ha'penny – and apart from flavouring, it probably had a medicinal value. The linseed-tea was soothing and effective, it was also slimy and revolting and my mother stood over me to make sure the last drop went down. The linseed, and the liquorice, were kept in the medicine cupboard, along with the permanganate of potash, little silver flakes that not only dissolved in warm water, but turned the gargle into a beautiful, bright crimson.

Mrs Watts had a greengrocery, and on a shelf, a few jars of sweets, and one of her aniseed balls, popped into the mouth, at the start of a needlework lesson, would last throughout the double session, and the sweet, impossible to chew, could be sucked undetected. There is a very vague memory of a hardware shop, owned by Mr Jury – and, in those days, hardware meant ironmongery. On the lower side of the Church was Brown's garage, standing back from the forecourt. Living in Gower Road, at the rear of the garage, there was a short-cut for Mr Brown to get to work, but it meant his treading a path on church land, and this he was allowed to do. However, in order that no right of way was established by him, the path he trod was closed once a year, but always on a Sunday, when the garage was shut; so the law was upheld at no hardship to Mr Brown — all very amicable.

Miss Peckham had a drapery shop, and next to her was Mr Butler's dairy, a double-fronted shop, in one window a large milk bowl, in the other a 'golden' cow. The International Stores was there, always shortened to the 'Inter', and I can remember a lad letting drop a coin through the grating – for all these shops had basements. Had that accident been mine, I should have walked sadly home to mourn my loss of wealth, but the boy was more of a stalwart, for he entered the shop to request a return of his money.

Mr Allen's shop had to be entered by a short flight of steps, and at the base of those, stood a display board, it was crimson, and on it, the head of a black cat advertising Black Cat cigarettes, for Mr Allen was a tobacconist as well as a hairdresser. The agricultural engineers, Rice Brothers, were next to the Public Hall, and the other side of it, The London Central Meat Co. with Mr Masters in charge. We children liked MacFisheries for on our way home from school, quite often the ice-van would be there, and the boys would bump each other up into the van to retrieve pieces of ice off the floor, passing them back to those waiting below. Ice cream may have been in short supply, but the ice-van was regular. Our mothers would have been horrified. Next to the fish shop was an ironmongery, Muzzell and Hilton, later, for a short while, Hilton and Clark, and later still, Horace Hilton Ltd. In its early days there was a wooden bicycle-rack on its forecourt, and it's on there I remember a few cartons of sale goods being displayed. In one of them were some unusual items, unusual to me that is, but my mother knew they were used in the Great War, and probably at other times, when money was scarce. They were metal cup-handles, able to be clipped on to a cup, if the china handle had broken.

We had a chemist in South Road, Mr Selby, and like Mr Grimsdick, he had started business in Sussex Road, at Number 18, in 1902, next to where the chemist's shop bearing his name stands today, and his faded advertisement may still be seen on the wall. Later he moved to a single shop in South Road, before extending his business to the adjoining one, which had been the gentlemen's outfitters for the Co-operative Society. Mr Lincoln had a butcher's shop, and on the Gower Road corner stood the shoe shop, Freeman, Hardy and Willis. A surfeit of empty shoe-boxes, would mean they would be stacked on the forecourt for any to take, and very useful we found them for our treasures, and for making beds for our dolls, but one day high spirited boys, going home from school, kicked them, with youthful vigour, along the road and, alas, never were they piled out there again.

From South Road we go into Sussex Road, and here was the Cross Roads post-office, taking its name with it when it later moved to the other side of the road. My only memory of the earlier one, is of being held up by my mother to post a letter; my better memory is of the Co-op cake shop, with Miss Morton behind the counter, for this area was Co-op territory with its many departments. It was the Haywards Heath Co-operative Society, until its merge with the Brighton Society in 1924, it was also where my mother shopped. The customer did not have to be a member, but could be with a £1 share, and then twice yearly would receive a dividend on all purchases within that six months, and for some, that dividend was a useful bonus for buying clothes or paying the doctor's bill. The Co-op's image today is totally different.

To the grocery department my mother and I went on a Saturday afternoon, with basket or shopping bag, for there were no shopping trolleys then and with no 'fridge or freezer, the amount purchased was small. Very little was pre-packed, tea was in a packet, as was cocoa, coffee in a bottle, custard powder in a tin, but cocoa and coffee could always be sold 'loose', though, as yet, we knew no 'instant' coffee. How dextrous were those white-aproned assistants, when serving a 'loose' commodity, for swiftly it was weighed, and then, quick as lightning, a cone made of stout blue paper, the product tipped in, and the top folded over.

On the other side of the shop, was the provision counter, where our rashers of bacon, cheese, butter, and sometimes a tin of salmon, were bought. The cheese cutter was a wire, bacon was sliced on a machine, and our butter cut to size and, with butter-pats, moulded into shape.

When our goods were paid for, the money, with a ticket of the amount spent, was put in a wooden cup, which went into place on an overhead wire, and a handle pulled, whisking it along to the desk, where it was removed, the change put in, and the cup sent back on its journey to the counter. The next shop along the road was Mr Turner's greengrocery, where a barrel of sawdust held grapes, and dates were cut as required, from a large block of them. Mr Tomsett had a boot and shoe repairer's business, in the next shop, selling sundries such as laces and polish, but it was the next shop that held our interest as children, for here was Harris's sweet shop. Mr and Mrs Stone were in charge, but sometimes Mrs Stone's mother, Mrs Harris, would serve, coming from the back region, through a bead curtain, and what patience they showed!! The shop was double-fronted, with cigarettes and tobacco on display in one window, in which we showed not the slightest interest, and sweets in the other.

The sweets, on the floor of the window, were arranged on saucers, each saucer having a white paper doyley. There were brown and pink burnt almonds, jap dessert, toffees, and pink and white sugared almonds, but these were sweets for adults, and we showed but a passing interest, as a shape of luxury in the future. Our greater interest was inside the shop, where on the counter was a fairly long display case, with a sloping glass lid, showing a mouth watering selection of ha'penny delicacies. There were sherbet-dabs, sherbet-fountains, sticks of liquorice, bars of nougat half pink, half white, liquorice boot-laces, "Best of All Toffee", wrapped in a waxed paper, liquorice pipes their bowls all aglow with red 'hundreds and thousands', and many other delights.

Spending a ha'penny was, for me, a time consuming business, for never could it be spent without lengthy deliberation, the pros and cons needed to be weighed up. Quite often the "Best of All Toffee" won, for I considered it to be good value for money. To my shame I remember once making my choice, paying, getting along the road, when a change of mind took me hurrying back into the shop, where it was patiently changed. There was chewing-gum on sale, and how that would have lasted, but it was forbidden by my mother.

That ha'penny was half of my weekly pocket-money, the other was for saving. As I got older my money rose to tuppence, a penny to be saved, and a whole Saturday penny to spend. What bliss. Older still, and I was to receive three-pence, but still the penny to spend, and tuppence to be saved, and to receive that princely sum, I was to do some dusting each week. I felt life was very hard. I remember one girl augmenting her pocket money, by doing house-work for an elderly couple, on Saturday mornings, but it would seem the boys were more enterprising. Some were delivering daily newspapers, some, on Saturdays, acted as caddies on the golf-course, while others on the same day, found employment as errand-boys, cheerfully whistling a current pop-song, as they pedalled their employer's trade cycle, complete with its deep wicker basket on the front. One laddie, on his way to school in the afternoon, would pop in to the weekly cattle market on a Tuesday, bringing his purchases to school to sell at a profit. I have no idea of his identity, but he's probably the wealthy owner of a chain of shops today. Of course, for some there was a yearly revenue from, "Penny for the guy" in November, and carol singing near Christmas.

Next door to 'our' sweet shop, Miss Mabel Scutt was there for baby linen and art needlework, further on Mr Knight had a house-decorators' business, Mr Cree's bakery was there, and Mr Dinnage had a motor-cycle and cycle depot, and there were many private houses in between.

On the opposite side of the road there was, as now, a public house at each end. Next to the Heath Hotel, was a sweet shop, Mr Swain's, his neighbour was the fish and chip shop, Mr Walder had a dairy, and next to him the post-office came from across the road, next Mr Brown's paper shop. Two shops adjacent to one another, were kept by Mr Cole, who sold bread and cakes, and was in the catering business. Later, Mr and Mrs Crocker were to take the premises as drapers and outfitters. We could buy drapery from Mr Chapman, and meat from Mr Pratt.

There were terraces of cottages in between the shops, all having gardens; one stood between the fish and chip shop and the dairy, the second between the dairy and the paper shop, the latter, Alma Cottages, may well have been built at the time of the Crimean War, and the third, Royal Cottages, stood between the Primitive Methodist church and the garden of the Sussex Hotel, and were the last to survive as cottages, being demolished in 1977, for the shops we see today.

It was to Mr Brown's paper shop that I had gone daily, one penny in hand, to buy the Daily News, later to become the News Chronicle, after a merge with the Daily Chronicle. The Mid Sussex Times, affectionally known as the 'Middy', was published Tuesday afternoons and cost tuppence, and it was my job to go to Mr Brown again. His little shop smelled of newsprint and the sweet smell of lather, for there was a wooden partition, not reaching right up to the ceiling, the other side of which, was a barber. There were weekly magazines such as Titbits with its green cover, Answers, in an orange cover, and Pearson's Weekly, which was a flowerpot red, all at 2d — tuppence. There were comics, too, some at a penny, others tuppence. I would have loved one, but like the chewing-gum, comics were taboo. There came a wonderful day, early in school life, , when a small laddie said to me at playtime, "I've got a big roll of comics at home, I've finished with. Would you like them?" Well, there was an offer not to be refused, and I started making plans of how to smuggle them into the home. Then, eagerly anticipating them, I waited. If an old gentleman out there somewhere,

Sussex Road.

happens to be reading this, and suddenly remembers a promise made, all those years ago in the playground — I'm still waiting!

There were other shops, not in actual shopping areas, but nevertheless offering a useful service to their particular part of the community. There was a grocery, Ashby Stores, on the corner of Western and Franklynn Roads, and nearby a greengrocery. A general shop on the corner of College and Millgreen Roads, and at the Commercial Square end of the latter road, a butcher's. New England Road, too, had its shops, as did Queen's Road. Mr Wood, being long established as a motor-cycle and cycle agent. So, although Haywards Heath was but a small market town, shops and businesses were bustling, and a few more will be looked at later when Boltro Road is visited.

CHAPTER 11

CHANGES

"The things which I have seen, I now can see no more"
William Wordsworth

Legend has it that an early resident of Butler's Green House, met a tragic end, when, being stabbed by a jealous husband, she ran from the house, with her child, through an iron gate set in the railings, across to the green opposite where both she and the child drowned in the pond.

As children we knew the pond, for it was not filled in until after the second world war, and there may have been more than an element of truth in the legend; it was her ghost, the Grey Lady we spoke off, but never saw. In conversation a few years ago with Mr Richard Moon, a present-day resident, he said that he had seen no ghostly appearance of the Grey Lady.

Certainly a small iron gate was there; locked, a stone slab tipped up against its base, and shrubs or trees growing behind it. It was known as the Haunted Gate, and supposedly had a curse upon it. It was made of hand-wrought Sussex iron, probably made locally from iron which might well have been dug and smelted in the area, and that lovely little gate was removed for scrap in 1942 as part of the war effort.

Its removal on June 17th: brought the B.B.C. to witness the demolition of "the gate with a curse on it", and I'm told the men formed a chain and passed the gate one to another, in order to break the curse. Perhaps that was when the Grey Lady ceased to haunt. Who knows?

War sees women weeping, and children having to be told that dad won't be coming home, and it's then that small losses sink into insignificance — yet upon returning home after the war, and learning of that little gate's ignoble end, I sensed a sadness, and, even now, wish it could have been spared.

As in other towns some private residences have been put to different uses, the boys' school, Parkfield, in Isaacs Lane, becoming Downland Park Nursing Home. Chownes Mead in Chownes Mead Lane, was, as a war-time measure, our maternity hospital, and the same war saw patients from Great Ormond Street Hospital, being evacuated to Elfinsward, at the Muster Green end of Bolnore Road. Elfinsward had already undergone one change, for in 1928, the house was given to the Chichester Diocese for use as a conference centre and retreat. After demolition in 1989, its site was used for our police headquarters.

In Bolnore Road was the Holy Cross Convent, an Anglican Community under the rule of St Benedict. The Community itself dates back to 1857, in London's Dockland, but a larger Mother House being needed, land, here, was purchased in 1872 and our Holy Cross Convent was being used by 1887, the chapel being built between 1902-1906. In 1979 the convent went on the market, with its four cottages, four acres of grounds, seven of woodland and nearly twenty five of farmland, for the sisters were moving to Rempstone Hall, near Nottingham. The guest house was converted to a residential home, Ashton House, the convent has become the headquarters for Sight Savers International. While the sisters were there, they chose not to use the mains water supply, but rather to have their water from an old sixty-foot well, that is in the grounds.

Some houses have become offices, Big Pennys in Wivelsfield Road, Heather Bank, now demolished, that was in Lucastes Avenue, Sandrocks in Rocky Lane, and our first hospital was in an Ashenground Road house from 1906. It was named Eliot House, Miss Eliot having, in her will, bequeathed £600 for a hospital. Seen to be an asset to the district, the adjoining house was purchased, but 1912 saw the opening of the King Edward VII (Eliot) Memorial Hospital in Butler's Green Road. Its closure came at the end of 1992, the Princess Royal Hospital having opened the previous year.

Oaklands, in Boltro Road, once a private house, has undergone change, but the road needs to be seen in its entirety. At the junction of Muster Green North and Boltro Road stands sixteenth century Old House, once Boltro Farm. Its farmland would have been split by the coming of the railway in 1841 and suffered further loss by subsequent development, as a result of the railway. More recently, some of its ground was acquired by the council for extra office accommodation, but that was after Oaklands ceased to be a private residence.

On that same Council acquired land, our Town Hall was built and opened in 1990. Early visitors to it, are seen photographed, sitting on the steps, they are children from Traunstein, the German town, with which we are twinned. The yellow postbox nearby was a gift from the Bundespost, the German equivalent to our Royal Mail.

That is recent history, when we come to Oaklands we see a house listed in the 1878 directory with Mr Harry Treacher as resident. In 1902 Mr James Bradford is there, a man receiving a knighthood in 1914 for his many philanthropic works, and he remained at Oaklands till his death in 1930, when he was 89. Sir James was responsible for the six almshouses being built in 1911 a short distance from the Dolphin public house, and each resident received a generous gift of money every Christmas. He gave the land for the building of the hospital next to the Bradford almshouses, along with over £300 to the fund which had been raised for the building of that hospital.

Surely he would have approved of his house becoming our Mid Sussex District Council offices, and of the County Library built there,

Showing archway and wrought-iron gates.

The canopy on the left is over main entrance to railway station. Station
Hotel or Goldings, opposite, now Zenith House.

and he would undoubtedly have been pleased at the 1997 sale of his summer-house, knowing that it would revert to its original use.

The archway at Oaklands entrance has gone, along with those tall, beautiful, iron gates. The accommodation has been, and continues to be, much enlarged, but the original building is still discernible, and the lodge remains.

Further down the road, was an access drive, a second one in Paddockhall Road, both led to Limehurst, a house which stood back between those two roads. The brickwork and pillars of the Boltro Road entrance, may still be seen today. Our Water Board offices were in premises built in 1938, and their red-bricked neighbour, was built for a general post-office, till another was built in the same road. It later became our telephone exchange, and, before being demolished in 1998, a sorting office for our mail. At the lower end of the road was a police house, the court-house and, on the corner, the police station. Of course there was no gyratory system.

Crossing the lower end of Paddockhall Road, we are in Market Place. Boltro Chambers, the garage and the bank buildings are there today, though the bank itself is closed.

The Station Hotel, with the Corn Exchange adjoining, had started its life as the Station Inn in 1843, but at one time, being kept by Mr Golding, was known as Golding's Hotel as well as Station Hotel, with a telephone number 8. With a re-siting of the station entrance, it again had a name change to the Hayworthe Arms Hotel. It had a chequered life: in early days it had served as a mortuary, following a rail accident; later it was to feed prisoners within the cells of the nearby police station; it catered for farmers from the market close to it. Overseas visitors would stay there, as would celebrities when filming in the area. It saw wedding receptions, and played host to many celebration lunches and dinners, and was renowned for its Saturday night dinner dances in the ball-room. It closed in 1984, and although it was summer time, had its last moments of splendour, bedecked with Christmas decorations.

It was converted to offices, Zenith House, and judging from the exterior, was a conversion beautifully done.

There was a wall next to the hotel, in front of which, on the road edge, was a horse-trough, and behind the wall, with its advertising hoardings, sheep pens, for it was then part of the market. Mr Bridges' little lock-up shoe-repairers shop was there, before moving further down to the market entrance, and then, standing well back, where now stands Caffyn's Garage, were four white cottages, nos.1-4 Market Place, their long gardens in front.

Next to them were the offices of T.Bannister and Co., with a pair of houses, before the market yard. The market was founded in 1866 by Mr Thomas Bannister, later his son being senior partner, and from small beginnings, grew to a site area of some eight acres, becoming one of the twelve largest markets in this country. Stock sales, Christmas fat stock shows, agricultural implement sales and much more were held. At the side of the market, cattle were loaded on to a special train, which stood on the railway siding and it was quite usual to see cattle and sheep hand-driven through the roads. A Boots the chemist manager once told me how a sheep made a dash for his open shop door, to be followed by the flock. Road transport was to take over for the conveyance of stock later on. Occasionally on a Tuesday, the weekly market day, a frightened animal would escape from the market to run loose in Boltro Road.

In August 1990, Haywards Heath ceased to be a market town, as the hammer fell for the last time on the bidding, but the name of Bannister lives on in Bannister Way.

Before we leave this area, mention must be made of our local Drill Hall, for it stood on the market site, until the building of new quarters in Eastern Road. But now, crossing over the road, we'll see what was on the other side.

The railway stables and two cottages for van drivers were there, for any delivery was done by horse-drawn vans. Opposite Goldings Hotel (later the Hayworthe) was the main entrance to the station; the steps, with brass handrails, leading up to the platform, and from the top step, on the left hand side, a door, half glazed, through which could be seen the station-master's garden. But the greater attraction for me, was the fact that some of the glass was coloured — my first introduction to coloured glass. Nearby was another item of interest, for the subway was there, and on the further side of that, was a wall. No ordinary wall this, for it had been built in ascending height, and its flat top being some nine inches wide, meant the wall was 'crying out' to be walked upon. I could never make it to the top, but I saw a boy do it, his arms flaying to keep his balance, for, gaining height, it was quite a drop down each side.

The first building at the lower end on that side of Boltro Road, housed an estate agent, Scott Pitcher, and the Assembly Rooms were at the top of the building. One or two shops ran a lending library, but there was no County Library, so when a school friend said to me, "If you could get your mum to give you a shilling, you could join a library that's just started", I was very interested, but thought it unlikely that I would get a shilling. But it was forthcoming, and both of us, clutching our money, ran down Boltro Road to those Assembly Rooms, for that was where it was held. Only fairly recently have I discovered it was a Townswomen's Guild undertaking. It bore no resemblance to our present library, but it was a library, and my friend and I were well pleased.

There were shops selling a variety of goods, outfitting, confectionery, drapery, dairy produce, ironmongery, and there was a hairdresser. Fruit and vegetables were sold by Mr Hales, his nursery being in Balcombe Road, now built upon with Fairfield Way, Oakhurst Lane, Orchard Way and Orchard Close. Let anyone enquire of my generation born in the town where somebody is living in that area, and the answer received is quite likely to be, "Oh, they live on Hayles' Nursery". Miss Eva Pannell had a photographic studio and, although her work is seen on local postcards, it was as a portrait specialist she was better known. Earlier Mr Douglas Miller had been in Boltro Road, the 1902 directory describing him as a photographic artist, and certainly any local postcard of his work seen today, displays his artistry. In the middle of those, and purposely left to the last, was the business of Charles Clarke (Haywards Heath) Ltd. That was the name of the business when I first remembered it.

Having served a printing and bookbinding apprenticeship, Mr Charles Clarke left his native Bideford in 1864. Six years later he set up as a printer and stationer in New Road, Haywards Heath, then an unmade thoroughfare, known to us today, as Boltro Road. It was in 1879 that he first published a Mid Sussex Directory and Year Book, and 1881 saw a local eight-page newspaper, selling for a penny — The Mid Sussex Times. He formed a limited company in 1917, and over the years, the company and the premises grew considerably, but in 1984, the stationery section was sold, and the printing section a year later. A great worker in the South Road Congregational Church, he laid one of the two foundation stones of that building in 1914, still to be seen today on the front wall of the now, United Reformed Church. He was also a benefactor to many good causes. His 70th.Birthday was celebrated with a concert given in the public hall, and the souvenir programme in my possession quotes, "May the sweet savour of our good deeds, lie well when we have gone over the last fence." Mr Charles Clarke went 'over that last fence' in March 1921, but the name lives on in the town.

The general post-office, built in 1915, was demolished in 1995. It was one of several that had served the town; the first, in a little general shop at Muster House, the second, at The Yews, and the third we have noted on the opposite side of Boltro Road. But on the other side where we are now, there was considerable change during the 80's and 90's, for apart from the post-office demolition, Waugh and Son, solicitors, the Cuckfield Rural District Council Offices and Albion House, went for office blocks. Today we see Cornelius House, Heath Square, to where Waugh and Co. moved, and Kinglsey House, our present Job Centre. The house Winkfield went, for part of the flats, Winkfield Court.

The red-bricked three-gabled office of the District Council, is worthy of mention, for it was an imposing building, put up in 1902, by Cuckfield builder, Mr Stephen Knight. At the top of its three steps was a huge, oak door, and, either side in the brickwork, a foundation stone. One had been laid by Major J.J.Lister J.P., the council's first chairman, who served for thirty-two years. He remains in my memory, as being one of the governors of the Girls County School in South Road, the other governor being Mr C.H.Ellis J.P. I can but hazard a guess at the other foundation stone, as being likely to have been laid by Mr Edward Waugh, for he was District Council clerk for almost fifty years. One engaged on its demolition is reported to have said, "It is one of the best built places I have ever seen, if not the best".

The house, The Yews, still stands on the top corner of the road, used now for a variety of purposes, all under the auspices of the West Sussex County Council. It took its name from two yew trees, one each side of the road, but one came crashing down in the hurricane-force gale which struck the south of the country in the early hours of the 16th.October 1987.

CHAPTER 12

THE WAY WE WERE

"The trivial round, the common task"   John Keble

Our footwear was leather, except for the canvas plimsolls with rubber soles, we wore for games. Boys wore black boots, and at the start of my school life in 1923, girls were still wearing brown boots, but the majority had shoes, and they were soon to become the norm. The boys wore socks with a turn-over top; the girls cotton socks, wool or lisle stockings, and, when older, rayon, an artificial silk. On my 21st. birthday I received a present of two pairs of real silk stockings. They were superb. While at school, boys wore short trousers, a long pair only when starting work at 14. There was no man-made fibre.

It was the milliners' hey-day, and had been for a long time, for hats were worn. Different fashions for women came and went, while men remained ever faithful to the bowler, the trilby and the flat, peaked cloth cap. Postcards viewed today of any football match in the past, will show the men spectators in hats and caps, and the few women in hats. Girls would be likely to have had a Panama hat in the summer, a felt or beret in the winter, but the beret was known as a tammy, short for tam-o-shanter. For a very occasional outing in her bathchair, my grandma would don a black, hard straw bonnet, tied under the chin with long, wide, black satin ribbons. When, as a child, I stopped wearing a hat, an elderly lady, looked at me, and said, scathingly, "Oh, and have you joined the hatless brigade?" It took the last war for women in the southern part of the country, to start wearing a head-scarf. Only once did I see a woman wearing widows' weeds, deep mourning, with a flowing veil of black crepe: and only once a woman with a face-veil, twizzled round and round under her chin to keep it in place.

Long hair, for girls, was sometimes plaited, either into one pigtail or two. Women's long hair, would sometimes be worn in a bun at the back of the head, sometimes plaited into a coil around each ear. Then came the fashion for hair to be cut, and we saw the bob, the shingle and the Eton crop, while most men and boys remained true to their 'short back and sides'.

It was not a throw away age, things, either made or bought, were to last, and even then their life was extended by mending, patching and darning. Frayed cuffs were mended, shirt collars turned, socks and stockings darned and the man of the house quite often did the family's boot and shoe repairs.

Our first cardigans were known as sports coats, and that may have been their original purpose, to wear on a round of golf, or to put on after a game of tennis. Part of a small girl's underwear, might well have been a sleeveless garment, known as a liberty bodice, and a woman's corset, she called her stays. Beach wear was a one-piece bathing costume.

Sundays saw us in our 'best' clothes, and for a walk on that day, my father took a walking-stick. I believe it was part of his Sunday attire, more than his having a need for it. Back home from the walk, it stood in a corner with a swagger-cane, a short stick with a metal head, and on the cane, a red cross, with which my elder brother had been issued when wounded in the 1914-18 war. It was not part of the issue when my younger brother was wounded in the next war.

As country children we knew what could be eaten from the hedgerow and what was to be left alone. Laurel leaves and deadly nightshade berries were taboo, but 'bread and cheese', the name given to the young fresh green leaves of the hawthorn, were good to eat, as were the haws — the fruit of the hawthorn, and the sour leaves of the sorrell quenched our thirst on a hot day. We picked flowers to take home — buttercups, a large variety of daisy we called horse-daises, bluebells, and being country children, we knew well <u>not</u> to pull the flower from the plant, so that the white area showed at the base of the stem: and there was one particular place in the park where 'tottle-grass' grew, which probably was totter-grass.

We collected anything — silver paper, matchboxes, foreign stamps, cigarette cards, 'bus tickets, orange papers. Then, in the early '30's, Nestlé's picture stamps appeared in their penny bars of chocolate, and by writing to the firm, a free album was obtainable. The fact that my friend and I had very little money, posed no problem, we went to the down-line station entrance, into the waiting room, where there was a Nestlé's chocolate machine, and every time a penny was inserted by a traveller and the silver paper and outer red wrapper, thrown down, my school friend and I pounced like a couple of hawks. Every picture stamp was so informative. Today it might be possible to find one of those albums among the ephemera of a postcard dealer. Incidentally, there was no platform ticket needed to get on to the platform and into the waiting room in those days.

Though it would seem the toilet-roll had always been there to serve its purpose, I know it was not so, yet the memory of its advent escapes me. Early on, with a brother working as a booking clerk for the Southern Railway, he would supply us with out-of-date excursion handbills, some an apple-green, others a delicate orange colour, and, cut in two, they served as toilet paper. Seen by visitors, they were thought to be superior to the squares of newspaper pierced at the top with a metal meat-skewer to take a loop of string to hang on a nail in their lavatories. By today's standards it sounds primitive, yet any paper was an improvement on what was told to my mother by an elderly lady who had lived in a very rural area, for her toilet tissue as a child, had been a dock leaf. There was another paper used within the home, and although <u>we</u> didn't have one it was quite usual to see a fly-paper. House-flies were much more prevalent than they are today, and the fly-paper was simply a strip of sticky paper hung up, and for unsuspecting flies alighting on it, there was no departure.

Where did the town's residents work? There <u>were</u> commuters, but employment of the greater number was local, either in the town or within cycling distance. Some were at Wivelsfield Green in the carnation nureries of Allwood Brothers, others at Charlesworth and Co.,the orchid growers, in Lewes Road, today's Orchid Park and Burma Close serving as a reminder.

Our builders were local firms, giving employment and taking on apprentices to learn a trade, and dressmakers were doing the same. Work could be found in offices, shops, hospitals, especially the mental hospital, due to its size, and hand laundries were a work place for some. There was always domestic employment and work for a nanny. Not until the 1960's did the Bridge Road Industrial Site and the one at Burrell Road come into being, but we did have one factory. It was the Thermogene Works, in Sydney Road, manufacturing a remedy for chest and rheumatic complaints. There were other Thermogene factories on the Continent. After the last war, our local one moved to another part of the country. The late Mr Albert Clarke, a director of Charles Clarke Ltd. and grandson of the firm's founder, being interviewed at the firm's centenary in 1981, spoke of being on leave in the last war, and going into Bombay, and of his surprise at seeing there, a packet of Thermogene chest rub manufactured here. Surely with the surprise there would have been, too, more than a twinge of homesickness.

Both the firms of Charles Clarke Ltd and George Hilton and Sons would have employed quite a workforce, and, at one time, so might the firm of Messrs. Jenner and Higgs who were millers and corn merchants. Under the Millgreen Road arch and into Balcombe Road, and there was Bridger's Mill, where, in 1856, Mr William Jenner had started his business. In 1880, a store was being rented in Market Place, near the station, for the laying up of corn and forage. It was thought that a spark from a passing railway engine at the rear of the warehouse, was responsible for the fire which completely destroyed it in 1915. Fire Brigades from Burgess Hill and Lindfield joined with the Haywards Heath one to fight the flames, and the Brighton Railway fire-engine came to protect the railway property. Crowds gathered hearing the fire-bells and shouts of "Fire! Fire!", and willing helpers, in the form of military, civilians, police and Boy Scouts did what they could to help. For a time it was found necessary to hold up the trains on both lines, owing to the scorching heat. Cars were removed from Golding's garage opposite, and the windows of Barclay's Bank were damaged along with some shop windows. This happened three years before my birth, yet I well remember people speaking of that conflagration, and it seemed those who had witnessed it, would never forget. By the mid 1960's the mill buildings in Balcombe Road had gone, and the area developed. Never again would rail passengers be able to look down upon the mill-pond and its swans, and remark upon its peaceful beauty. Bridger's Mill lives on in the Close of that name.

There was little money about, and I have no idea what shop prices were early on, for children are more interested in the food, than how much their mum gave for it. But in 1932 Vida knicker elastic was 6d. a card of 3 yards, and electricity was charging a summer quarterly rate of 9/-, a winter one of 17/6, while 120 units were supplied free of charge, and any in excess were one penny per unit. In 1936 little savoury biscuits called Krax came on the market at 3d. for a large packet. In the same year, a friend was having a costume made, the coat costing £2. 2s., the skirt £1. 5s., a total of £3. 7s. In the same year her husband was buying a pair of flannel trousers for 12/11, a cap for 2/11, and he, too, had a suit made, costing him £4. 4s. In 1938 electricity units fell from 1d. to ¾d, and the number of free units available was raised to 140.

Advertisements were showing us the scrawny, scruffy, Bisto Kids; a cheerful looking Mr Kruschen was leaping around, having taken Kruschen Salts — "enough to cover a sixpence every morning"; Beechams pills apparently were "worth a guinea a box"; and Elasto would "lighten our step." It says much for the advertising at that time, that some can be remembered sixty years later. I wonder if the present TV commercials will come to mind to a future generation, after that length of time.

Under the Millgreen Road arch and into Balcombe Road,
a view seen by rail passengers.

CHAPTER 13

WAR YEARS

"There never was a good war" Benjamin Franklin

In 1932/33 the entrances to the railway station in Market Place and Station Road (Clair Road) were closed, and the station re-sited to where it is today. The subway was extended, the platform reconstructed, and automatic signalling installed. The 1930's saw both residential and commercial development. Looking at the Church Road end of South Road, after Tar Path and the graveyard, there were no shops for some third of a mile. The house, Brent Eleigh, stood there until 1980, being demolished for the shopping precint, but the frontage of Brent Eleigh was taken in the 1930's. Trees and beautiful rhododendrons in flower were uprooted, and there were lofty bonfires. It was 1934, and beautiful weather, when Miss Stevens, the head mistress of the Girls County School, which stood next to Brent Eleigh, thought to have the literature lesson on the lawn at the rear of the school. The building of shops on the adjoining site was in progress as we trooped outdoors with our chairs and books. Barely had the lesson started, when one of the workman gave a wolf-whistle, and our alfresco lesson was quickly terminated!

That block of shops was a Sainsbury enterprise, opened as South Parade. A brick on the lower side of the block, bears the initials J.B.S. —John Benjamin Sainsbury was chairman and governing director of the firm, at that time. That group of shops gave us Cornish Ltd. tobacconists; Clarkes Bread Co; Sainsbury Ltd; Woolworths; Boots Ltd. the chemist; the Scotch Wool Shop; and Freeman Hardy and Willis, moved there from Sussex Square. Woolworth's had their red fascia board, with its gilt letters, F.W.Woolworth & Co. L^{td}. and it was from there, my mauve darning-mushroom came, it cost 3d. from my first pay-packet. I have it still and it has served me well over the years.

A year later, in 1935, the lower block was built, Fludes next to the graveyard came later, on a separate single site. One of those original businesses is there today selling household linen and much more. It was opened by Mr Edwin Baldwin and is now run by his daughter and grandson. The shop doubled its size in 1967, when the flat above was incorporated into it. There is a counter, and staff to serve, offer advice and discuss any query the customer may have. Long may it remain.

The year 1936 saw the opening of shops built on the site of the former County School, and Bateman's opticians remain as being there from the beginning. When the Council School was closed in 1938, its demolition was partial, the rear portion remaining as workrooms for the firm, G. Hilton & Sons, its frontage taken for shops. It was also the year my father died and the income into the home, was the widows pension of 10/- per week. There was no money for me, though still at school, I was over the age of fourteen, and could have been a bread-winner. My mother wasn't told about the school holiday abroad — I kept quiet. There was no feeling of deprivation for I knew what we couldn't afford we didn't have.

With the sound of the church-bells still echoing, on that lovely morning, the 3rd: of September in 1939, the nation heard the words of its Prime Minister, Mr Neville Chamberlain, "I have to tell you…that this country is at war with Germany". Fairly soon we were to hear an unusual sound — the siren. Out in the garden my neighbour was irate, "Now there's a time to come, — just dinner-time!" We were to become accustomed to the siren's wail, along with gas-masks, the blackout, rationing and ration books, identity cards, clothing and petrol coupons, A.R.P. wardens, evacuees, and much, much more. From the B.B.C. we had the Home Service only, the Forces Programme coming a little later. Announcers introduced themselves by name; Vera Lynn (later a D.B.E.) was singing; and, at least, a couple of comedians were making us laugh — Tommy Handley and 'Lord Haw-Haw', although the latter 'joker' didn't even realise he was doing it! We became used to seeing posters entreating us to "Dig for Victory"; to "Be Like Dad, keep Mum", and telling us how, "Careless Talk Costs Lives.

These were all normal to the nation, but in Haywards Heath, our aluminium was taken to Finch's Yard in Commercial Square; and I recall only two places for tank-traps, some on the forecourt of what was then the Westminster Bank (now 'Nat West'), and some in the front garden of No.8 Haywards Road; there were others, of course, as there were static water tanks, but the sole one of those in my memory now, is the Gower Road one, near the twitten. Our iron railings, taken for 'the war effort' have left ugly reminders, in the town, of their removal. Nobody asked politely, "Would you mind, frightfully, if we took your railings?" There was a war and they were needed to supply furnaces for raw material, in order to make quite different objects, and we had already learnt the word, commandeered.

Gas masks in this area, had been issued from the Council School and the Public Hall. and ration book renewal, is remembered once, as being in the Gower Road Church Lads Brigade Hall. There were other venues for different parts of the town.

A Ministry of Food had been established, and our Local Food Office was in Commercial Square, with a Potato and Carrot Division in Lewes, till its move to Boltro Road. It was there, at Barton Chambers, opposite Oaklands entrance, that I spent several very happy years as a ledger clerk. In Haywards Road, near where Iceland now stands, a temporary building was erected as a British Restaurant, where coupon-free meals were served. No longer needed for that purpose, it became, in the 50's, our Youth Centre, till the opening in 1962 of the Albemarle Centre.

The L.D.V. (Local Defence Volunteers) was formed, to become, later, the Home Guard, more often remembered today as Dad's Army. We also had troops in the town, and to cater for their free time, forces canteens were opened. St Richard's Church, Perrymount Road Methodist Church, and the Congregationalists in South Road all opened their church halls for this purpose and ran the canteens. Undoubtedly The Church of St Wilfrid would have played a part, but had no hall at that time. All had good canteens, but because my knowledge is of the South Road one, it is that one I will describe.

It was opened at short notice in 1940, and 'manned' by the women of the church along with helpers from the Sussex Road Methodist Church: it closed in 1945. Its opening time daily had been from 6.30pm to 9.30pm, with the Sunday start at 4.30 and it was open 365 days a year. It was roughly estimated that half a million sandwiches, a quarter of a million cups of tea, as well as innumerable cakes, buns and tarts had been made and served, one helper alone making 10,000 tarts. Everything was sold for a 1d. each. The padre of one of the military units stationed locally wrote, in his letter of thanks, of the Christmas Day openings and the wonderful time given to the men. The visitor's book of the church at that time gave eloquent testimony of the gratitude of the men and women who had made use of the canteen. It was placed on record that no case of bad conduct in any form occurred, during the whole time the canteen was open.

My boss thought that my work could be classed as a reserved occupation and therefore exempt from the call up. Not having discussed it with me, he had no idea of how I felt, so taking a train to Brighton, I walked down Queen's Road, into the Oddfellows Hall, where I volunteered for the W.A.A.F. I loved the work while in the W.A.A.F.and friendships forged at that time are still being maintained today. One night I was on my way back to my billet, the train was running very late, the crammed-full waiting room, stuffy, and to get a breath of air, I went out onto the platform. It wasn't long before a very young Canadian soldier started a conversation with me, and I discovered he was a very worried young man. It appeared he had a mother who 'ruled the roost' in the home, and she had impressed upon him, that he was to bring a wife back from 'home'. In fact, they were the last words she had uttered, as he left. It was evident that 'she who must be obeyed' was causing him a problem, so much so, that on Haywards Heath station platform, in the blackout with kit-bag and all, he said, "I suppose you wouldn't marry me, would you?" He was absolutely right, I wouldn't. What a humorous, pathetic little story!

We had a few bombs dropped. A stick of four high explosives fell in the Bentswood area, damaging houses. A stick of bombs also fell across Ashenground Wood, the last exploding in the rear garden of a house on the west side of Haywards Road, damaging houses in that road, Wood Ride and Park Road. Windows in Ashenground, Gower, Sussex and South Roads were broken; my mother and I, in Gower Road, were fortunate, needing only to pick up everything that had been blasted off the shelves in the shed. A young man walking through the recreation ground suffered a spinal injury when a bomb dropped there.

In 1944 the Germans launched a long-range weapon, an erratic, diabolical thing, known as a flying bomb. It carried a ton weight of explosives, and went at a speed of 350-400 m.p.h.; it was pilotless, jet-propelled and exploded when it crashed. They were set on course from Nazi-occupied Europe to London and, being stationed in the north of England, we never saw them, so coming out of hospital, I was questioned before sick leave was granted whether my home was in the path of these flying bombs, and knowing that leave would be stopped if I answered truthfully, I lied, "No, they miss Haywards Heath". Getting back after leave I found myself very much in demand by the R.A.F., who had by some means, heard about this WAAf who had been on leave in the south, and they wanted to know about these pilotless bombs. I had little to tell, but enjoyed the popularity while it lasted.

The war ended in 1945; only it doesn't ever end for some, while others never came home. Their names were added to war memorials, their loved ones left to grieve. We will remember them.

On upper side of church in South Rd, Jeffries' sweet shop,
Godfrey, baby linen and James' electrical goods.

The Carnaby Pew.

CHAPTER 14

THE TOWN GROWS

"- - - and go on till you come to the end"   Lewis Carroll

Six years of war, with a following period of recuperation, halted both residential and commercial development, but gradually both increased. Demobilization had brought home men wishing to start married life, and others who had married in wartime, all needing houses. Temporary homes were erected, prefabricated buildings known as 'prefabs' , council-owned houses were built and in 1953 Ash Grove was constructed as a self-build enterprise, as was Southdown Close, three years later.

Larger shops were to take the place of smaller ones on the upper side of the South Road Congregational Church (now United Reformed) in 1963. Sainsbury's, in their original South Parade store, were needing larger premises, so the shop, one time Rice Bros. further down South Road, was purchased, and until needed, became the Carnaby Pew, a coffee bar for young people, being sponsored by the District Council of Churches. In 1971 Sainsbury's were building, on that demolished site, a self-service store, and we were becoming used to the word, 'supermarket'. The opening of Clair Hall meant the demolition of our Sussex Hall — one time Public Hall, Sainsbury's neighbour, and in 1974 the supermarket was extended on to the adjoining site. The town, still growing, meant even larger premises were needed, and the store in Bannister Way was built, and opened in 1991, and since extended. Budgen's shop occupied the former site in 1992.

Boots, the chemist, had previously vacated its original shop, for a move to larger premises in what was once Timothy White's, but 1981 saw them building further down South Road on the site where Brown's

Garage and Chapman's greengrocery had stood. Both W.H.Smith and Woolworth's have moved to larger shops, as have Milwards.

In South Road the shopping precinct, Orchards, opened in 1982 as Priory Walk. A multi-million pound project, it was built in a triangle formed by South, Hazelgrove, and Church Roads, and apart from Fine Fare's supermarket, now Marks and Spencer, consisted of 35 smaller shops and 31 flats. The car park necessitated the demolishing of houses in Hazelgrove Road, Toledo, Grove Villa, Elsinore, Selsfield, Lyntonville and Gordonville all being razed, as were Hilton's work-shops, the last remaining part of the former Council School. A re-designed and modernised Hilton's Dept. Store formed its South Road frontage and the store re-opening, at the same time as the opening of the precinct, was a celebration of 100 years of Hilton trading in the town. The Haywards Heath Town Band led a procession, prior to the arrival of a vintage Rolls-Royce bearing celebrity openers, Faith Brown and Tim Brooke-Taylor, who were to compère fashion-shows during the afternoon and sign autographs throughout the day. The store closed in 1987, and those of us who remember its earlier days, still mourn its passing.

Often unnoticed, there is a sundial on the side of the building that is now Marks and Spencer, but very noticed are the two clocks presented by the local Rotary Club in 1983, when celebrating 50 years of its activities here. 1984 saw more autograph signing, when June Whitfield and Terry Scott paid us a visit for the opening of one of the shops.

As a town we are not over-endowed with sculpture, so John Ravera's delightful 'Family Outing' erected in 1985, is rather special. Also in the same year our Boltro Road General Post Office was demolished, and 1986 saw another, opening in Orchards, and the close of the Sussex Road sub post-office at Joytoys. The precinct was given a facelift in 1998.

There have, of course, been closures, Horace Hilton Ltd. ironmongers, electrical and heating engineers in Sussex Square, a business of long standing, closed in 1980, and in Sussex Road, the Co-operative Society, here since 1894 and much modernised over the years, finished trading in 1987.

A growing population meant an increase in both road and pavement traffic, and the '60's saw a long traffic island in Sussex Square, nicknamed The Queen Mary. Also in 1960 South Road's forecourts were lost, to a road-widening scheme, the most noticeable being at the Congregational Church, where fence, double-gates and garden disappeared.

The roundabout in Sussex Square was installed in the 1970's, and it was about this time that concern was being shown at the narrow width of the pavement which skirted the churchyard. So congested had it become, that pedestrians were being forced to step out on to the busy A272. To widen it would mean, not only the removal of the boundary hedge and railings, but also the lych-gate, which had been erected in 1909, by a local builder, Mr Arthur Purvey. It would necessitate, too, the disturbance of several graves and a reburial of the remains, and, understandably there was strong opposition; but a transistory court overruled the objections and, screened from the road, the graves were dug, and there was a reburial in the presence of funeral directors and the then vicar, the Rev'd Roy Hicks. The pavement was widened, and the Burgess Hill firm of Norman and Burt, made an excellent job of re-erecting the lych-gate and constructing the stone wall, completing the work early in 1971.

The town has grown around its early houses. To name but a few, Great Haywards Farm House in Oakwood Road, off the Muster Green, dates back to between 1420 and 1450; while Little Haywards in Haywards Road (one time Little Haywards Road), Old House, formerly

Boltro Farmhouse, at the top end of Boltro Road, and the Balcombe Road Mill House are all about the same age.

At Butler's Green, Steeple Cottage, sometime chapel, barn, court-house, is shown on the 1638 manorial map, but may well be much older. Harlands Farm is dated, at least early 1600's. Its farmlands were lost in 1955 to the Harlands/Penland housing area, and the light industrial estate in Burrell Road. A grammar school took some of it in 1958, and the Dolphin Leisure Centre in 1976. So the town continues to grow, modern property seen as if endeavouring to usurp that of long ago.

Life is very different today. No electricity meant no television, no internet, no hi-fi equipment, no fax machines, no electric typewriters or cleaners. 'Fridges, freezers, washing-machines, spin-driers and tumble-dryers, all unheard of; so was frozen food, instant coffee, pizzas and quiches. No ball-point pens, or disposable nappies, no man-made fibre; and plastic was a word unknown, though we did have celluloid, and, later, bakelite; space travel was nothing but science fiction. We married first and lived together after, and surprise was shown, should anybody get divorced. There was no by-pass surgery, joint replacements, or National Health Service, and we wouldn't have thought of wiping our noses on paper. Road rage? My thoughts go back to a peaceful summer evening, when my father's boss, Mr Jim Muzzell, took my parents and I for a car-ride. I had, and still have, no idea where we were, but the memory remains clear, even now, of a little girl running from a house on one side of the road, and looking neither left nor right, dashing in front of our oncoming car, to her mother, waiting on the opposite side. We

Two rural views of Harlands Farm

discovered the brakes of Mr Muzzell's car, were very good. The frightened mother screaming, held tightly on to her crying child, and then suddenly realised an apology was necessary, and looking up, said to our driver, "I am sorry. I am so, so sorry." The car, had an open top, and in my mind's eye, I can see now Mr Muzzell standing up in the car raising his trilby and saying, "That is quite alright madam, quite alright." Road rage? We didn't know it!

Words had a different meaning, coke went on the fire, a joint was for Sunday lunch and crumpet toasted for tea, hardware was sold by an ironmonger, and anybody gay, was the life and soul of a party. At school we learnt there were 240 pence in a pound, 12 pence made a shilling, and 24 made a coin called a florin — not so today, girls were taught to darn — no longer needed, and we all learnt the atom could never be split — not true.

We can indeed say, with L.P.Hartley, "The past is a foreign country: they do things differently there"[*] and that is something every generation can say. Now I must finish my letter to Haywards Heath.

• from :L.P.Hartley's prologue to 'The Go-Between.'

- - - - and now, Haywards Heath, having put on paper a few of my memories, I will finish your letter as promised. From your eight farmhouses, nine cottages, two inns and one windmill, set among gorse and bracken in 1800, you have today, a population figure of around 22,130, and that's quite a growth. Our lives, too, have altered, being revolutionized by the coming of electricity into both home and workplace. Money was in short supply, yet we were happy, something my young friends today find difficult to understand.

You now offer more facilities, and you are a better place in which to live, — and yet no longer are little children able to play unaccompanied in the park or recreation ground, or walk the woods and fields; neither can windows be left open when not at home, or doors remain unlocked after dark. Is it any wonder my generation sometimes says, with Shakespeare, 'O! call back yesterday, bid time return. But that's not your fault, its the way things are. Once, another town did beckon me, and I was sorely tempted, but I could never leave you.

Lilian Rogers.